W9-BBV-469

BENEDICT'S WAY

BENEDICT'S WAY

An Ancient Monk's Insights
for a Balanced Life

Lonni Collins Pratt
Father Daniel Homan, OSB

LOYOLAPRESS.

CHICAGO

LOYOLAPRESS.

3441 N. ASHLAND AVENUE
CHICAGO, ILLINOIS 60657

The English text of the Rule of St. Benedict is a personal translation derived from the original Latin and using other Benedictine sources as references. Because the ancient text is Latin, English translations may vary.

The Scripture quotations contained herein are from the New Revised Standard Version Bible: Catholic Edition copyright © 1993 and 1989 by the Division of Christian Education of the National Council of the Churches of Christ in the U.S.A. Used by permission. All rights reserved.

Cover and interior design by Jennifer Mindel
Cover art © Steven Rothfeld/Tony Stone Images

Library of Congress Cataloging-in-Publication Data

Pratt, Lonni Collins, 1953–
    Benedict's way : an ancient monk's insights for a balanced life /
    Lonni Collins Pratt, Daniel Homan.
        p. cm.
    Includes bibliographical references.
    ISBN 0-8294-1787-7 (pbk.)
    1. Benedict, Saint, Abbot of Monte Cassino. Regula. 2. Spiritual
    life—Catholic Church.
    I. Homan, Daniel, O.S.B. II. Title.

BX3004.Z5 P73 2000
255'.106—dc21   99-046790

Printed in the United States of America
    06 07 08 SHER 10 9 8 7 6 5

to
Mom who meant to give her little red-haired
baby girl strength and faith that would
help me walk through my world. Instead
you gave me wings.

to
Rich. Though the singer is silent, the song goes on.
The music and the memory remind me that you
know what I meant. I didn't know eternity stood
between May and October.

—LCP

to
Dad and Lisa, wait for me.

to
all the young people who have touched my life and
to our Sunday morning community of friends at
St. Benedict Monastery, a source of such love.
Thank you.

—DH

CONTENTS

Acknowledgments

There are always people who make sacrifices so that other people can write books. My husband, David, is one of those people. He has relentlessly loved me and supported my writing habit for many years. I am endlessly grateful.

Thank you, Jim Manney. When you pulled my article out of the pile so many years ago, I got lucky.

This book could not have been written apart from the monastic community of St. Benedict Monastery. They are like John Denver's "Matthew" for whom "love was just a way to live and die." Thank you for teaching me so much.

Finally, though words inadequately express my gratitude, thank you, Dan. Thank you for all you are and for who I am because you are my friend. Thank you too for not laughing, or running, when I mention yet another book.

—*LCP*

My mom lives in Southgate, Michigan, and my dad lives in heaven. There is a big difference. But I am grateful to both for the gift of life and for all they taught me by the way they have lived. They nurtured and encouraged my Benedictine vocation. You can hardly find parents like mine today.

My brothers and sisters, so young when I left home, have always been a source of strength and encouragement. I'm grateful to them.

The Benedictine brothers with whom I have lived, worked, and prayed—some for short periods and others for almost forty years—have inspired, challenged, and loved me. I have been blessed by them.

Father Mike Green has been my friend and brother in community longer than anyone. He is a cherished companion.

Mary Kay Cummings has ministered with us Benedictines since our days at St. Scholastica and then in our retreat house for thirty years. I have seen her work miracles with her faith. She has my deep admiration and gratitude. You couldn't find a better friend.

Finally, I thank my coauthor, Lonni Collins Pratt. She encouraged me to get into the writing profession and believes deeply that the Benedictine way of life still speaks in our time. I am in awe of her talent and appreciate her friendship and support.

—*D*

What Is a Retreat, and How Could One Be Valuable to Me?

Chances are, the pace of your life is white-hot fast. There's a lot to do every single day, and you are expected not only to do it but also to do it well. If that isn't enough pressure, you have to cope with the deluge of information that assaults you at every turn.

Our time is complicated. But that doesn't keep us from thinking about the big issues in life. Does my life matter? What am I here for? Am I a freak accident in the gene pool? Is God real? Does God care about me? Does God care about what matters to me? Am I making the right decisions? Am I becoming the person I want to be? Will this pain ever end?

A retreat is time set aside for you. Maybe you'll relax or sleep. But if you stick with it, you can be sure that the big questions will start coming to mind. We can only push away the questions, doubts, and fears for a little while. And eventually we all face the same questions. A retreat is time set aside in which you open yourself to those bigger questions. It is time away from what is ordinary to you. It usually means leaving your home or office and going someplace quiet and isolated. A park bench works, a tent in the woods, a hotel room, a retreat center. But if getting away isn't possible, you can make a retreat in your favorite chair with the television off. You can sit under a tree or on the deck or at the lunch table in the cafeteria. You can carve out a few minutes propped up in your bed just before you fall asleep.

What do you do? Most of us think and pray while making a retreat. Others just rest and take long walks. There is no wrong way. It helps, especially if you're new to the idea of a retreat, to have a guide. A book like this one is a guide. Sometimes at retreat centers you can find a spiritual director to act as your guide. This book is a resource for a retreat you make on your own, without a spiritual director. This book is your companion.

For many people, the thought of taking a full day, a few days, or a week away from everything just seems impossible. But with determination you can set aside a few minutes every day to make a retreat. During this period you'll read this book and possibly read from the list and suggestions we provide. You can follow the chapter from beginning to end in each retreat time and allow yourself to experience a little taste of solitude. It doesn't need to be complicated. Get alone. Read the book. Reflect. Be silent and restful with God.

When you do this for a while, you might be interested in making a retreat of a half day or a few days. But a good way to start is to set aside a little time each day to think about your life. One very common way to pray is to think about your life while consciously considering yourself in the presence of God. You just say, "God, I am with you right now, and these are my thoughts, my questions, my dreams, and my hurts. . . ." St. Benedict tells his monks that if they want to pray, well then, they should just pray. Just do it.

We need to find ways to slow down our minds and find peace. We need to sort through the many complications of modern life. We need to become the people we are created to be. All of these things are helped by the act of making a retreat, whether it's in an easy chair or at a monastery.

Who Was St. Benedict, and How Is He Relevant Today?

Benedictine spirituality is enjoying a surge in popularity. It's hard to say what started it. A few years back a group of Benedictines soared to the top of the music charts with the CD *Chant*. Books about spirituality often include sections about the Benedictine method of prayer, called Lectio. Kathleen Norris drew attention to the Benedictine life in her book *The Cloister Walk,* a national best-seller. Monasticism has become trendy, along with just about any ancient source of wisdom.

The Rule of St. Benedict (RB) was written by St. Benedict, who is often credited as being the father of Western monasticism. He wasn't given this title because he was the first monk or because he started the first monastery, but because, with few exceptions, Western monasteries use the Rule that he wrote about a millennium and a half ago.

St. Benedict was born into a confusing world much like our own. Things were changing fast. People wanted something solid to hold to, something that would steer them in the right direction, something that could be trusted. But their world was propelling forward, and they had no rudder.

As we all know, you can't steer a boat without a rudder. Benedict's world was an uncertain, chaotic one, hit by wave upon wave of turbulence. In this way, Benedict's time had much in common with our own. Life was a battle to make sense of all that was happening, a war for personal meaning and significant values. We aren't the first generation fighting this battle. Those who have gone before us just might have something to say that will be helpful to us, something relevant, timely, profound. We have found that Benedict is all of that.

Benedict was Italian. Between A.D. 410 and A.D. 476, the Roman Empire collapsed. Benedict was born about the time of the official fall of Rome, A.D. 476 (his traditional year of birth is 480), when Romulus Augustulus, the last emperor, was deposed. This event was so traumatic that it shook the underpinnings of civilization. The church splintered apart from political, cultural, and theological battering on every side. Chaos rocked Christianity, and the situation seemed to be worsening with every passing day.

Into the chaos of the time appeared Benedict, a man with a simple plan for order, sense, and peace. The Rule of St. Benedict gathers together the strands of its Eastern origins and the Western ideas of Augustine on community. It takes the monastic traditions passed down and synthesizes them into a single tradition, now called the Benedictine tradition. This tradition of taking the old and the new, of taking what is cutting edge and what is perennial to the human spirit, is typical of Benedictine spirituality.

Benedict called his document a "little rule for beginners." He did not view his contribution to monastic literature as anything spectacular. He wrote, "This is advice from a father who loves you." Compared to other rules it is indeed a little rule. The entire text is seventy-three very short chapters, which, when printed, fit on no more than one hundred pages. It is remarkable for its brevity and clarity.

"This message of mine is for you . . . if you are ready to give up your own will, once and for all," wrote Benedict. "Therefore we intend to establish a school for the Lord's service. In drawing up its regulations, we hope to set down nothing harsh, nothing burdensome. The good of all concerned may prompt us to a little strictness in order to amend faults and safeguard love."

Sensible, simple, sturdy, difficult—we don't think Benedict would mind that we use these words to describe his Rule. He would be pleased that the essence of the life he prescribed remains strong medicine for a society still very much in need of healing.

Authors' note: For our comments on the history of the RB, we rely on the excellent work of the many Benedictine scholars who composed the introduction to RB 1980: The Rule of St. Benedict in Latin and English. *For what is possibly the most succinct, readable, and definitive history of Benedict and the RB, we highly recommend it.*

What Is a Rule, and How Could One Be Useful?

A rule is a set of principles and actions around which we organize our lives. Everyone lives by a rule. Many, if not most, people do so unconsciously. To clarify, any of these definitions could describe a rule:

- Values that determine what is most important and direct your everyday actions
- Habits that are consciously formed for the sake of physical, emotional, and spiritual health
- Guidelines that assist in making ordinary choices every day
- Goals for personal growth and improvement that you reach by acting on a specific plan of action

As part of a "rule," most of us do certain things daily—shower, brush our teeth, eat three times, go to work, complete chores, relate to spouse, family, friends, and coworkers, study, relax, exercise, engage in sports or hobbies. We have discovered that these activities give us the kind of balanced life we are striving after.

However, despite the desire to have a balanced life, sometimes things seem very much out of balance. We are more than a collection of water, bone, and muscle. Our needs go beyond seeing to the basics.

A rule, in the sense used by St. Benedict, means a plan for living with others in a certain way. It is the glue of monastery life. It is the common denominator. It is the understanding that exists between the members of a monastic community. Despite personal differences, inclinations, and preferences, a rule determines how individuals will respond and behave and live together.

Benedict's Rule for monasteries provides a basic unity to the Western expression of monastic life. There have been many other rules written for monks, and all have fallen into disuse. In the fifteen hundred years since Benedict first composed the RB, it has become the means by which contemporary monasticism remembers its Eastern origin, and it has become a unifying force for contemporary monks and nuns.

The durability and survival of the Rule is impressive and commends it as a source of spiritual insight. But can a document written that long ago speak to our lives today?

Maybe the question itself reveals more about us than we realize. Such a question is based on the assumption that our age and our culture are preeminently unique, that we experience life and the human spirit in some way that has not been experienced before.

If we accept such an idea, we establish a basic principle that sounds something like this: I can gain no help or insight from any source outside myself and my culture. In this view, the experience of shared humanity is without value.

But does the experience of living support such a notion? Not at all. It doesn't take us too long to realize that we need others. None of us learns much of anything without help from others. If the answers to the difficulties and challenges we face were found exclusively within our own culture, we would all surely be happier and better adjusted. It has been long held among seekers of wisdom that the aged, the ancient, and the enduring are fertile ground for wisdom.

Tradition is a vehicle by which truth and faith are transfused into each generation. The church herself stands squarely on the tradition of Jesus as articulated to us by the testimony of men and women who lived two thousand years ago.

Even if we accept that something ancient has value, what do we gain by reading and considering anything called a rule? The word *rule* is something of a problem for us. We don't like the authoritarian sound of it. We expect a book of laws. The Rule of St. Benedict is best understood as wisdom literature. The insights of the past provide a basis for understanding ourselves and our world. They are nothing but dead letters unless we integrate them fresh into the experiences of our own lives. Practice is essential to embracing spiritual wisdom.

The RB should not be approached as legislation. Don't read it with a literalistic ear. Read it as you would good poetry or allegory. Mine it for depth of imagery; think about how the words written by Benedict might apply to a different time and situation. The Rule does contain rules for organizing daily life inside a monastery. But rules are also a way of expressing wisdom, love, tradition, and the fruit of experience gained in the school of hard knocks. Ask any parent.

The Transforming Power of Benedict's Rule

Benedict's message is for all of us, not just monks. And it will transform us if we are ready to give up our own way, if we have come to realize that "Thy kingdom come" means "My kingdom go"!

Monasteries are places where people go together to God. They vow themselves to a shared life. They take the vows of obedience, stability, and conversion of life (celibacy and poverty are assumed). The Rule allows strangers to find harmony together and to live in a common understanding.

But all of us spend our lives with others. Married or single, in a family or on our own, there is still a multitude of people with whom we are spending life. They might come and go as we move or change jobs, but we will still be surrounded by others. Our common life matters. Our common life with every other human being on the planet matters. Monastic life is a powerful illustration of this.

It's true that we are not all monks or nuns. We're assuming that you, our reader, are not a monastic. However, each of us, if we are to survive with some self-respect intact, if we are going to sustain our ability to love, trust, and give, will need to find shelter for our battered souls. How do we stay tender in such a tough world? How do we remain true? How do we continue to feel? How do we keep getting up morning after morning and putting one foot in front of the other?

Without being overbearing or arrogant about it, monastics have something to tell us about how to keep our broken stumps of hearts open to God and others. Like all people of prayer, they are the light of the world that Jesus talked about. Light permeates, but it's silent.

What is the silent witness of monasticism? Revolution. Nonconformity. Resistance.

In the life they chose—in the radical approach to prayer, celibacy, possessions, justice, and much more— Benedict told his monks to intentionally go against the cultural norm. For most of us, that can be translated into challenging the American Dream and all the trappings of our culture. The spirit of the monk is the spirit of Christ. That monastic spirit is not the exclusive possibility of those who live in monasteries. We can all be revolutionaries. We can all resist the clanking of the cultural bell and heed instead the resounding sound of the monastic one that calls us to prayer and service. If that's our intention, we will find a marvelous companion in Benedict.

There is a defense-shattering authenticity to Benedictines who have lived with the Rule. People who have lived with the Rule become irresistible people, compelling people. When meeting one, you have the sense that you're talking to someone with substance, a real person and not a stick person without insides. You get the feeling that someone is listening, really listening, to you for the first time in your life.

The Rule of St. Benedict—and, indeed, the gospel of Jesus Christ upon which it stands—will gradually replace the automatic rules, or codes, that have haphazardly formed us over the years. As the new rules are written into our lives, astonishing things will happen inside of us. We will become people who are more open to others. We will become people who are fortified for the hard times and who can remain tender when we have to get tough. We will become people who have the courage to love, even though Jesus showed us that loving will be costly and put our lives at risk. We will become people who cease to fear the risk and are no longer easily shaken. We will become *people.*

This is what the gospel is about—"in the world but not of the world." Belonging but not buying into the party line. Benedict gives us a way to implement the gospel in our ordinary lives. He helps us think like Jesus people. He helps us react to life like people who know the living Christ.

How Can I Do My Own Retreat?

L et's say you've decided to make the reading of this book a retreat. Or, after reading the book, you decide to make a retreat. We can help you plan this venture. This section deals with the practical stuff—where, how, when, and so forth.

Where? It depends on your preferences, of course. Enriching retreats have been made in boats, hotel rooms, tents, cabins, beaches, monasteries, campgrounds, guest rooms, garages, conference centers, college dorms.

Any place that is quiet, where your solitude will be respected and you are set apart from your daily routine, will work as a retreat site. Check out local monasteries, convents, and retreat centers. Ask around your church for suggestions. If your initial inquiry does not lead you to a suitable place, you should consider a cabin, a camper, or the spare room of a friend who will leave you alone for a few days.

Plan in advance. If you are married or living with others, be certain to talk with them about your plans. It's important that your retreat not cause undue hardship on anyone else. Carefully consider when your work and family schedule is light enough that your absence will not create too much difficulty. Despite responsibilities and relationships, almost any person can go away for a few days without the bottom falling out of the world.

If necessary, ask a friend to be available to help with your family if an extra ride is needed, a meal needs cooking, or the lawn needs to be cut. Plan to do the same for them. Also, tell someone you trust about your retreat plan and the hopes you have for it. When you return, talk to that person again about what happened and what it meant to you. Your life and spirituality do not occur in a vacuum; the experience will be more meaningful if you share it with someone close.

Also plan what you'll take. Keep it to the bare essentials. Take clean, simple clothing suitable for climate and setting. Do not pack makeup, jewelry, cologne, and so forth. Avoid taking razors, blow-dryers, curling irons, or anything that will take too much of your time. Plan to keep personal hygiene simple and easy. Towels, a sleeping bag, a pillow, and maybe a reading light should be packed also. Bring a Bible, a prayer book, and one other book for spiritual reading. Do not bring work, homework, your briefcase, pictures, letters to write, stamps, your personal organizer, cell phone, beeper, or laptop computer.

For your comfort and health, remember medications and consider items such as a small fan or heater, bottled water, and groceries if you have to provide your own meals.

If you are responsible for cooking your meals while on retreat, keep it simple. Bread, vegetables, peanut butter, rice, or pasta will see you through and are easy to prepare.

It's helpful to have a basic, uncomplicated schedule in mind and hold to it. If you stay at a monastery or retreat center, the schedule will most likely be set for you.

Of course, your schedule will vary depending on how much time you have and what you're comfortable with. Generally speaking, you want to begin a retreat when you're fresh and rested, so early morning is a good time to start. Spend some time thinking, praying, and journaling. Take a walk or get a little exercise. Read a little. If you're eating (some people fast on a retreat), try doing so in silence or with music playing. Other elements to include in a retreat are Lectio Divina, creative writing or drawing, and periods of silence. Seek a rhythm that moves you from prayer to contemplation to action and then back to prayer.

Here's a schedule for an all-day retreat that you can use or adapt:

6:00 Meditate on the morning prayer and reading.

7:00 Eat breakfast, clean up, get some simple exercise (such as a walk or swim).

8:30 Read, pray, journal, draw, sleep—whatever is restful and connects you to God.

11:30 Meditate on the noon prayer and reading. Then eat lunch, clean up, and spend time in silent meditation.

1:00 Take a nap.

2:00 Participate in some kind of work, do something creative, read a book, pray, talk to a spiritual director, sit in a chapel, sit in the woods.

6:00 Pray the evening prayer, eat dinner, clean up, read a newspaper or magazine, take a walk, prepare for the next day, and pray a centering prayer. Do something restful to wind down for sleep.

9:00 Pray the night prayer. Go to bed whenever you become tired, but don't go to bed too late if you want to follow the schedule and be up by six in the morning. Time before sleep is often good for journaling and reading. Such activity would keep some people awake. Experiment so that you can fall asleep easily.

Even if you've never kept a diary or journal, be sure to take along a notebook so you can record ideas, insights, plans, whatever comes to you. It will also be helpful in discussing the retreat later with someone else.

How to Use This Book

This book is our attempt to enliven the Rule of St. Benedict for those who have never read it, as well as those who are already familiar with the Rule. There are thirty short chapters here. You can read one each day for a month, or three per day for ten days. Or you can read straight through the material as you would any book. Adapt the material and set your own pace.

For example, if you decide to make a retreat for three days, you could begin working with the book ten days before your retreat, work through ten or twelve chapters while on retreat, and then finish the book in the next week or ten days after your retreat.

If you're using the book for a group retreat, you can adapt it in the same way or simply begin the book together, work through as many chapters as reasonably possible while on retreat, and then finish it individually or meet together weekly in a small group to discuss it.

Small groups will find much here to discuss and reflect on together. It would be helpful if small-group members also select a book from the reading list to read together simultaneously.

Perhaps you're simply looking for a book about living a balanced life, and you want a little help. You won't find a better guide than St. Benedict. Read each short chapter and spend a little time working through the introspective material at the end. Give the material a chance to sink in. Don't rush yourself. You can read it on the bus as you go to work or school, on your lunch hour, or while the kids are napping or outside playing. The book is written so that something can be taken from each chapter with only a short investment of time. The last section of each chapter contains questions for you to think about, ideas for action, and a prayer.

The thirty chapters build on core Benedictine values of humility, obedience, sacred rhythm, and relationships. Work and prayer are strong Benedictine values. We explore these values by relating them to various topics. The topics selected are not exhaustive of what Benedictine spirituality is about. By dipping into this book you will have a taste of St. Benedict and Benedictine spirituality.

Central to the Rule and running through the text of this retreat is the idea of listening. The first word of the Rule is *listen.* In a circular fashion, we also begin and end with listening in each chapter. It is a theme you will come across often. The listening Benedict refers to is something more than the sense of hearing.

Resources to Enhance Your Experience

Two supplemental books are necessary if you're going to get the most from this personal retreat—the Rule of St. Benedict and the Bible (or the New Testament and Psalms). Liturgical Press in Collegeville, Minnesota, has an inexpensive copy of the Rule, and they are very good about shipping books speedily. It is best if you use an edition that numbers chapters and verses sequentially rather than giving readings for each day of the year. We strongly suggest the one mentioned above.

Use whatever Bible translation appeals to you. The New Revised Standard Version, New Jerusalem Bible, and New English Bible are all fine translations. When we refer to Scripture texts, we cite the New Revised Standard Version.

We make suggestions along the way for various spiritual disciplines. These are the ones we think are most important for the purposes of a retreat:

- Morning and evening prayer (See chapter 2.)
- Prayerful journaling
- Lectio Divina (See chapter 23.)

For the discipline of morning and evening prayer, we suggest you consider one of these volumes: *Work of God: Benedictine Prayer,* edited by Judith Sutera, o.s.b., or *Pray without Ceasing: Prayer for Morning and Evening,* by Joyce Zimmermann. Others are listed among the resources in "Suggested Reading."

A simplified one-volume copy of the Liturgy of the Hours is available at Catholic bookstores. It is not written in inclusive language, which makes it problematic for the contemporary mind. With practice, you can learn to mentally replace the gender-specific language with more meaningful pronouns and phrases—in personal prayer and reading. This won't work for everyone. However, if you're able to do it, it is a good way to make use of some otherwise excellent prayer resources.

If you do not have a prayer book that organizes the Psalter for morning and evening prayer, you can do as Christians and Jews have done for centuries—begin reading and praying the psalms as organized in Scripture, a few each day.

In *The Message,* Eugene Peterson has translated the book of Psalms in such a way that it grips the mind of contemporary readers. For those who are familiar with the Psalms, his translation can bring fresh meaning to familiar texts.

The monastic day, as Benedict organized it, pivots on the "offices" of prayer. Monks rise early and punctuate their day by praying the psalms. The number of offices and the times vary slightly, but most monasteries have five to seven offices of prayer. Benedict called this prayer the "Work of God." Monastic prayer centers on the psalms. We learn from monastic prayer that our emotions, whims, and situations are less important than we think. Regardless of what is happening, the monk shows up for prayer day after day, all the days of his life. There is nothing supernatural inside the monk that enables him to do so. He just puts his feet into his shoes and walks to the chapel. How he feels about it is not relevant. When it is time to pray, you pray. Period. You don't have words? Don't know how to address God? Not a problem. The psalms are full of words, words that we make ours when we pray them. This kind of prayer anchors us.

While reading this book, allow the psalms to be the voice of your prayer. It will lead you into more personal prayer, but always begin with the Psalter. Many versions of the Psalter are dated and rather archaic; find one that is meaningful to you.

If you've read other books about spirituality, you have probably encountered the term *Lectio Divina* and have heard it attributed to the Benedictine tradition. We have included an important chapter about Lectio. It is at the heart of Benedictine spirituality, and we encourage you to give it a try. Lectio Divina is, simply stated, the slow, prayerful reading of the Bible. When you engage in Lectio, it is your soul's core that meets the printed words on the page. This is not intended to be anti-intellectual. There is a place for textual studies of Scripture, and such studies are very beneficial. But Lectio is not Bible study or any similar intellectual endeavor.

A related spiritual discipline that will enhance your experience is prayer journaling. There is no wrong way to do this. Just write down your response to what you read in this book or in Scripture. Write about your experience in Lectio; write about your feelings. If you make a decision to begin something or end something or do something differently, write about it. Some people take to writing prayers, poetry, and journal entries quite naturally. Others struggle to get words on a page. Don't make it an impossible task by setting unrealistic expectations. Write half a page a day in a spiral notebook. Almost anyone can manage that. The important thing is that you are honest with God in these scrawls on a page; that's what makes it prayer.

Benedict was a man of his time, and his Rule is not written using inclusive language. Benedictine women have long lived with the Rule and come to love it. Whenever we deal with very old writings, the cultural norms of the author will need to be patiently forgiven and understood. There are potentially troubling passages in the Rule if we are not able to forgive and understand that Benedict, despite his efforts to resist his culture, was still shaped by it in ways that he could not have recognized—just as we all are.

We suggest that you read short passages from the Rule while working with this book, but it isn't necessary. Selections from the Rule are included in each chapter. These will provide you with a strong sense of the power and beauty of Benedict's Rule.

Who Are the Authors?

This seems like a good time to introduce ourselves.

Who are we? Father Daniel Homan, O.S.B., has been a Benedictine monk for almost forty years. He is also a priest and the prior at St. Benedict Monastery in Oxford, Michigan. He has led youth retreats for almost thirty years. He's known there as chief grass cutter and ditchdigger, but those aren't his only passions. He's pretty passionate about hockey too.

Lonni Collins Pratt is a Catholic laywoman. Her informal association with the monastery is one of friendship. She visits as often as possible for Mass with the monks, a cup of coffee, or a few days of retreat. Lonni is married to David Pratt; they have five children (Michael, Scott, Shelly, Andrea, and Michelle) and two grandchildren (Gina and Chelsea). Lonni has been a writer and journalist for most of her life.

Our writing collaboration was born out of our common interest in Benedictine spirituality. We share the conviction that one does not have to be a monastic to be Benedictine in some sense. The Benedictine vision has something important to teach us, all of us. We think the strength of our writing collaboration is this common vision combined with our obvious differences. Fr. Dan brings a lifetime of following God in the Benedictine tradition as a professed monk. Lonni is new to Benedictine spirituality, and her life is as non-monastic as yours. But the words of St. Benedict speak to both of us deeply.

Both of us enjoy solitude too. A retreat experience presents the opportunity to step back from the harried pace of life, to not only rest but also think and pray about the things that matter most. There's so much noise in our lives. Each of us cherishes the times we have in solitude. We believe in retreats.

The retreat journey you are about to take incorporates stories from our lives. You may or may not make an actual retreat of this book. We realize that many of you will simply read it cover to cover or pick it up now and then and read a few pages. Either way, one side effect of reading the book will be that you'll get to know us a little and—we hope—feel that we've become friends. Feel free to write us in care of Loyola Press, and they will see that your correspondence is forwarded. We would enjoy hearing from you about your experience with this book.

Benedict wrote that whenever we set our hands to a new endeavor, we should pray. Good advice. And as you begin, keep in mind Benedict's first word of the Rule: *listen.*

1

LISTENING

The Rule of St. Benedict

Listen carefully, my children, to the master's instructions, and attend to them with the ear of your heart.

—RB Prologue:1

Other Voices

The Rule of St. Benedict opens with the word . . . listen. Properly understood, this is the key to this whole spiritual teaching. A monk should be above all a listener. So indeed should every Christian. . . . The whole spiritual life of the Christian . . . is a process of listening to God, "inclining the ear of the heart," as the Rule says. This image of the inward ear, the ear of the heart, shows us that our listening is not merely an intellectual or rational activity; it is intuitive, springing from the very core of our being; where we are most open to God, most receptive to the word he speaks. We have to be very quiet and still within ourselves, very alert and attentive, if that word is to resonate properly in our innermost depths.

—Cyprian Smith, o.s.b.
The Path of Life: Benedictine Spirituality for Monks and Lay People

Lonni

L isten is the first word of the Rule. It is the core of Benedict's Rule and what you might call its last word as well. The listening St. Benedict refers to has little to do with being able to physically hear, or not hear. It is a matter of attending to the lessons of life, the lessons that come our way from the "masters"—those who have gone before us—the older, the wiser, the enduring.

When Benedict refers to a master, he means someone who has endured in the faith and therefore is able to lead by example, not simply by word. We might call such a person an example or teacher.

But Benedict is no literalist, and to approach the text in that way misses the spirit of Benedict himself. Benedict tells us to listen to life with our hearts open. A master for us might be a person. It could be a book. Scripture. Liturgy. Eucharist. Maybe a song, a movie, or lunch with a friend. It's everyday stuff and everyday people.

I arrived for Mass at St. Benedict Monastery early one weekday morning. Mass was scheduled half an hour earlier than usual because some of the monks were taking a truckload of junk to the dump and wanted to be there when it opened. The monastery was several months into a building project, which had left the interior gutted like war ruins.

In the corridor outside the chapel, I ran into the oldest of the monks, Brother Benedict, who is eighty-five. His voice sounds like gravel and velvet mixing. Being hugged by Br. Ben is like being caught in a vise. His kisses are sandpapery, his demeanor somewhat gruff.

The corridor is where we often talk going to and leaving Mass. We don't talk much; Br. Ben puts his hand on my shoulder, and we smile at one another. Every now and then, he will cross the chapel to where I am. On those occasions, he takes my hand, looks into my face, and asks if I am OK. It is a common enough gesture. Lots of people ask the question. But it's different with Br. Ben. He means it. He is a monk of few words, yet his faithfulness to the monastic vows for his long lifetime speaks volumes. This is someone whose life I want to hear.

Our friendship has been shaped by the culminated hours we have sat together in the chapel across from one another in silence, just the two of us. Our being together before God has forged a remarkable bond.

During the eucharistic liturgy when we all say, "Grant us peace," Br. Ben is about one pace behind the rest of us. Because he's mostly deaf, I don't know if he hears that his ancient, soulful voice echoes us like the prophet's voice clear and true. We finish saying, "Grant us peace," and then Br. Ben rumbles, "Grant us peace."

It is the prayer of a man who has lived long enough to know that peace is not the rule in our world, and so he pleads for it, day after day, on behalf of all of us. His endurance, stability, strength, and sheer joy are all lessons for me. Important ones. In his praying he is also a master. I don't just hear his prayer; I *feel* his prayer for peace. When my life gets crazy, I remember his prayer and breathe a bit easier, no matter how far I am from the chapel and Br. Ben.

Despite his hearing deficit, he communicates with ease, when he wants to. The advantage of his disability is that no one who doesn't want to talk to him ever bothers, and only those who genuinely care make the effort. Br. Ben's talking is never more than a sentence or two rattled or roared at you with one of his all-knowing smiles and a twinkle in those ancient eyes. In like kindness, replies are best kept to short sentences spoken in the loudest voice you can politely use in a monastery.

In the shadows of predawn we met in the corridor. He smiled, crushed me in arms made hard from a lifetime of cattle tending, and said, "Mass is early today." I nodded, then asked loudly, "How are you?" (He had been down with a cold.)

He lifted his arms, making a great circle with them and drawing my attention to the ruins around him. His hands were raised palms up, in a kind of desperate petition. He rasped a distinctly old, Italian, male grunt of resignation. He wasn't happy with the changes happening in his home. That's how he was.

I understood. "It must be difficult to have your home torn up this way," I replied.

He nodded. He shrugged. Then Br. Ben took hold of my arm and said, "Let's go to Mass."

His prayer-saturated life has shaped him into someone who cannot be shaken by gutted shelters and falling ceilings. He was telling me something important. No matter what kind of ruins you stand in, keep moving, keep doing what you must do, keep showing up every day. Haul yourself before God no matter what.

Br. Ben is a master. This crusty old monk who lives among his brothers is an icon through which I see St. Benedict and Benedictine spirituality more clearly. He is kind and tough; he is practical and prayerful; he is hospitable, loving, and affirming while holding tight to the monastic virtue of solitude.

Masters are usually unsettling to hear. It takes a singular attention from us. Hearing with the ear of the heart is what Benedict wants us to learn. But it doesn't come easily. We'll have to hold in faith to a conviction that human beings really do have an inner ear. It will take us a lifetime to get good at hearing. We have to keep at it. If we do, masters will teach us to listen with our hearts.

Going Inward

Think about a time when you listened to a situation, a person, or a reading, and something seemed to speak through it. How did you recognize the voice? Did you trust your inward ear?

In what situations do you now hear God speaking? What hinders you from listening? In what situations would you like to hear God speak? Have you been listening, expecting to hear God?

Try to keep your inward ear attuned to the rustling of God today, in the people you meet, in your experiences, in what you read, see, hear, touch.

Holy God, I believe there are masters of vision, masters of peace, masters of wisdom and joy and love for me to hear. But my inward ear has been dulled by all the nonsense it hears and the cacophony of my world. I don't know where or how to start, but teach me to listen and help me believe I can actually hear you. Amen.

2

PRAYER

The Rule of St. Benedict

First of all, every time you begin a good work, you must pray to God most earnestly to bring it to perfection. . . . Let us open our eyes to the light that comes from God, and our ears to the voice from heaven that every day calls out this charge: *If you hear his voice today, do not harden your hearts* (Ps. 94 [95]:8).

—RB Prologue:4–10

Prayer should therefore be short and pure, unless perhaps it is prolonged under the inspiration of divine grace. In community, however, prayer should always be brief.

—RB 20:4–5

Other Voices

A spirituality without a prayer life is no spirituality at all, and it will not last beyond the first defeats. Prayer is an opening of the self so that the Word of God can break in and make us new. Prayer unmasks. Prayer converts. Prayer impels. Prayer sustains us on the way. Pray for the grace it will take to continue what you would like to quit.

—Joan Chittister, O.S.B.
In a High Spiritual Season

These people who pray know what most around them either don't know or choose to ignore: centering life in the insatiable demands of the ego is the sure path to doom. . . . They know that life confined to the self is a prison, a joy-killing, neurosis-producing, disease-fomenting prison.

Out of a sheer sense of survival they are committed to a way of life that is unselfed, both personally and nationally. They are, in the words of their Master, "light" and "leaven." Light is silent and leaven is invisible. Their presence is unobtrusive, but these lives are God's way of illuminating and preserving civilization. Their prayers counter the strong disintegrative forces in American life.

—Eugene Peterson
Earth and Altar: The Community of Prayer in a Self-bound Society

"O God," I said, and that was all. But what are the prayers of the whole universe more than expansions of that one cry? It is not what God can give us, but God that we want.

—George MacDonald

Lonni

I like to think that my failure to pray is a result of my busyness. I'd rather not consider it an indication of a hard heart, a heart refusing to hear God, refusing to hear others. But I can't escape the fact that my heart is callused. I know it when I cross the street because of my reaction (or lack of one) to the pile of homeless humanity cluttering the sidewalk. I know I am callused when I look away from a kid with drug-dazed eyes or I resist speaking to the person in the wheelchair.

Every time I refuse to hear, I grow less capable of hearing. That's how the calluses got there. It probably started before I knew what was happening.

My granddaughter Gina is five months old as I write this. Her hearing appears to be fine, but the amazing thing about Gina is that she hears what most of us don't. She hears the silent people. I don't have to say a word for her to hear me. I walk into a room, and she turns her head and looks at me. She hears my presence.

If I am napping in the same room she's in, she won't sleep because she feels my presence even though she can't see me. No matter how quiet I try to be, she knows I'm there and gurgles, giggles, and coos at me.

When my oldest daughter, Shelly, was a teenager, she had an eye trained for me too. In an instant, she could find me in a crowd at her softball game or concert. It didn't matter how big the crowd, how much noise, or how much distance was between us. She would find me effortlessly. I asked her once how she did that, and she looked at me as if I had just asked the most stupid question she'd ever heard. "I don't know. I just know when you're there." She shrugged.

Failure to pray will harden us and deafen us to God's presence. Prayer trains us to hear God's presence in our world, in all the people who silently walk into the rooms of our lives, and in all the words not spoken. Our prayerlessness is not about how busy we are or about all our good intentions gone wrong. It is about the state of our callused, hard-of-hearing hearts. The irony is that the thing we are resisting is the only cure for the ailment: prayer.

St. Benedict doesn't say much about prayer methodology in the Rule. Keep your prayer simple and to the point, he says. If you want to pray, well then, pray.

Simplicity is the antidote to the single thing we seem to blame for our failure to pray: busyness. If prayer is simple, if all we have to do is do it, then we can relax. It can be done in the shower or in the car. It can be done alone, or we can gather our families and friends. We can pray and walk, pray and exercise, or we can just sit still, do nothing, and pray. We don't need formulas and methods.

I believe we have an instinct for God. Sensing God's presence comes as naturally to human beings as sensing my presence comes to my children and grandchildren. When our hearts are filled with loving someone, we grow increasingly aware of that person. That is what happens when we pray. We begin to spot God in the caravan of life.

Going Inward

Begin to notice how often you pray and what hinders you from praying. Write a note to yourself in your calendar, or post a note on your bathroom mirror or car visor that simply says, "Pray." Consciously remind yourself to pray every day for a week. After a week, do you notice any difference in how easily prayer comes to you? Do you notice any difference in your attitude?

Commit yourself to morning and evening prayer. This might seem ambitious to you, so start small. Pray for a few minutes right after you get out of bed and for another few minutes before you fall asleep. Stick to it. Add psalms and the Lord's Prayer to each morning and evening office of prayer. Purchase a prayer book from the list in the back of this book.

It takes twenty-one days to form a habit. It might be helpful to write down the times each day or ask someone you trust to ask you about your progress in prayer.

Sample morning prayer:

Dear Lord, before I hit the ground running, I pause to be claimed again by you, to be reminded of what matters most, to offer myself for your service in whatever opportunities you give me this day. Thank you for another day and for a safe night passed in your care.

Sample evening prayer:

Dear God, soon I will sleep. Grateful for this day with all its joys and all its complications, I give myself to your loving care and am happy to rest in your love. Forgive me for my errors, my neglect, my hard-heartedness of today. Lord, have mercy. Amen.

3

WORK

The Rule of St. Benedict

Idleness is the enemy of the soul. Therefore, let there be specified periods for manual labor as well as for prayerful reading. . . . When they live by the labor of their hands as those before us did, then they are really monks. Yet, all things are to be done with moderation on account of the fainthearted.

—RB 48:1, 8

Other Voices

Work is meant to be holy endeavor. Such a vision forms the context for our own daydreams about what we might contribute to our own and one another's work so that it can be more fulfilling for ourselves and more beneficial to others. This vision insists that our work matters, not simply as a means to make money, but as an expression of faith and being. . . . Benedict treated the human body and human work as fundamental ingredients of the holy life. In his view labor was not only dignified, but conducive to holiness. Prayer was more likely to take root in our lives when anchored in practical work.

. . . Benedict's Rule illumines three basic principles about work enfolded in the context of prayer:

1. vocation, being called to what we do
2. stewardship, taking care of what is given
3. obedience, serving one another.

—Norvene Vest
Friend of the Soul: A Benedictine Spirituality of Work

Dan

B rother Albereic discovered he had cancer only a few months before the illness ended his life at age ninety-eight. The hard news didn't change his life much. He did not stop working until two months before his death. Br. Albereic continued to cook for his brother monks. He gardened, mowed the lawn, and joyfully served the community.

I remember when I went to visit him during the last days of his illness. His face came alive, his smile reached his eyes, and he said, "Danny, you came all the way to see me?" He made me feel as if I handed him the hidden treasures of Atlantis.

Our participation in labor is a tool in God's hand by which we are created, by which we help create. Br. Albereic's work shaped him into a man of prayer, a man who was good at loving his brother monks. Think about that. In the hours spent pushing a lawn mower, stirring soup, shoveling snow, polishing a table, pulling weeds, Albereic was being worked on by God. We are too. We do very ordinary things, and God breathes life into the act. God breathes life into us.

Work also stands as a constant reminder that we are not alone in this world. There are others to think of, there are things to get done, and there is a kingdom to build. Work turns us outward, lifts our heads, straightens our shoulders, and extends our hands to others.

This is a higher vision of work. "Pray and work" (*Ora et labora*) is the Benedictine motto. Work is not less holy than prayer. It is not the dread enemy that prevents us from having fun. It is not a way to get to the weekend. Work is holy. Work and prayer are partners. We need both contemplation and action. They complement each other by keeping our feet firmly rooted in the soil of life and our hearts strongly fixed in the love of God.

It takes discipline and determination to tackle work with a spirit like Br. Albereic's. As we are faithful to our work, we are faithful to all the lives we touch, and we are faithful to a vivid holy vision of ourselves. Work joins us to the substance of creation. Work graces us with dignity. Work joins us to God.

Going Inward

As you cross paths with people today, think about how their work is important to you and to others. What would happen if every person who is working at a job today really believed that what he or she does is important, not just for making a living, but for building the kingdom of God?

Begin to pray as you start work and when you are finishing for the day. This prayer need not be complicated. Simply turn your mind toward God for a few moments. Pay attention to any impressions or feelings that come to you.

Even in difficult situations, our work is a means of experiencing God. What good thing might come out of a difficult situation at work?

Take time to think about how your work is influencing who you are becoming. What skills have you acquired? What important lessons have you learned? How have you changed?

While you are making this self-guided retreat, keep a journal to keep track of your responses, feelings, and progress. Be sure you date each entry. Don't feel that you have to write very much. A few lines may be all you require. Your journal is also a good place to write down your prayers, prayer requests, concerns, and so forth.

God, you care enough about me that my work is important to you. You love all of us enough that there is inherent dignity in the labor of our lives. Remind me that I am your partner in creating the world you are designing—and that I am your partner in creating myself. Help me to cooperate heartily, and give me insight into the value of my work. Amen.

4

STABILITY

The Rule of St. Benedict

Do not be daunted immediately by fear and run away from the road that leads to salvation. It is bound to be narrow at the outset.

—RB Prologue:48

The workshop where we are to toil faithfully at all these tasks is the enclosure of the monastery and stability in community.

—RB 4:78

If after a while the visiting monk wishes to remain and bind himself to stability, he should not be refused this wish, especially as there was time enough, while he was a guest, to judge his character. . . . He should even be urged to stay so that others may learn from his example, because wherever we may be, we are in the service of the same Lord and doing battle for the same King.

—RB 61:5, 9–10

Other Voices

Nothing frightens us more than the prospect of having to hold to a particular course, come what may. This deep instability in our nature corrodes our marriages, our religious vocations, our friendships, our work. We are prey to our passing moods. . . . At times we have reason to wonder whether we possess such a thing as a single, unified personality. . . . To remedy this situation is one of the primary aims of the monastic life, as it is all Christian life . . . there is an abiding sense that however things may be going, even though they may not seem at the moment to be going particularly well, he is nevertheless in the right place, doing the right thing with the right people. The passing moods cease to matter; they are recognized as transient and ephemeral, like clouds in the sky.

—Cyprian Smith, O.S.B.
The Path of Life: Benedictine Spirituality
for Monks and Lay People

The spiritual value of stability lies in commitment. Like everything else in monastic life, stability works best when it is wholehearted, without escape hatches or preserves of autonomy.

—Columba Stewart, O.S.B.
Prayer and Community: The Benedictine Tradition

Lonni

When a friendship of many years crashed apart, all I wanted to do was get out of town. I talked to contacts in several states about job openings in publishing. After a little while, I decided that Colorado was the place for me—and proceeded to try to convince my husband.

But my husband comes from a long line of people rooted in one place. His soul is attached to Michigan. So when I hauled him off to Colorado, he looked around and, intelligent man that he is, noticed immediately that Colorado, while a high and interesting place, is not wet, green, and lush. It is not surrounded by large bodies of water and pocketed inland with swamps, lakes, streams, and ponds at every turn the way Michigan is. He likes that about Michigan. He took a deep breath and began taking pictures of every dribble of water he could find.

After a while, I offered to pull the car over and let him get out to take pictures of puddles. I couldn't bear to part the man from his home, so we stayed in Michigan.

Monks, and farmers, live in cycles. They are attached to what goes and comes around again. They enter into a sacred redundancy morning upon morning. Our culture doesn't put much value on the familiar. Those who hold to routines, who go to the same job year after year and stay married to the same person for a lifetime—well, they aren't the stuff that movies are made about.

There are times when we stay in a situation that is clearly not good for us. It is destructive and not at all life giving. That's not stability; that's foolishness. Stability calls us to remain in difficult situations but not in destructive ones.

Benedictines take a vow of stability. They know that eventually another monastery is going to look better. Another way of life will sound appealing. They will question themselves. They will question the people who make choices that affect their lives. They will someday wonder about every single choice they have ever made.

And when that happens, they will remember the promise of stability made before God, their brothers, their families, and their friends. Despite circumstances, they will stand still, they will shut up, and they will out-last the doubts. They will outlast the darkness that corners all of us every now and then. You could call it holy stubbornness.

Hikers in the Tarryall region of Colorado are advised that if they become lost while in the vast wilderness, they should stay where they are and stop wandering. Hunker down and wait to be found. Stability calls us to believe that if we stay where we are, God will find us.

Going Inward

There's a well-known indicator of stress that most of us have heard about. This evaluation tool lists various events that cause stress, and the more of them you've experienced recently, the higher level of stress you're likely to experience.

Interestingly, many, if not most, of the stress indicators involve change. A move to a new house or city, a marriage or divorce, a layoff or new job, the birth of a child, the death of a loved one, a major purchase, a career change—these are all indicators of stress.

Certainly all of the changes we face aren't avoidable. People die, spouses leave, and companies downsize. But a lot of the things that cause stress seem to happen at our own hand as a result of the choices we make.

Is there a change you're considering now? If you take seriously the Benedictine virtue of stability, how would it affect your decision? How might the same virtue improve your attitude in a difficult situation?

What is most stable in your life? How have you found stability? How does your faith act as an anchor?

Stable and loving Father, change and upheaval sometimes seem to be the rule. I know that I crave what does not change. I crave love, friendship, dignity, and security that lasts. If I am going to know this kind of stability, though, it will have to begin with me. Anchor me deep. Hold me hard. Teach me to stay put, to be courageous, and to outlast any doubts that assault me. Amen.

5

CHASTITY

The Rule of St. Benedict

No one should pursue what they judge better for themselves, but instead, what they judge better for someone else. To their brothers and sisters they show the pure love of family; to God, loving fear; to their leaders, unfeigned and humble love. Let them prefer nothing whatever to Christ, and may he bring us all together to everlasting love.

—RB 72:7–12

Other Voices

The whole concept of purity is currently not much in favor, probably because it was used, in the immediate past, in a way that seemed to make the noble virtue of chastity both unattractive and unattainable. The major effect of the discussion of chastity was a sense of guilt; it inspired dread rather than generosity. . . . The monastic emphasis on purity of heart . . . explained in terms of singleness of purpose, inner undividedness . . . in this case the image is seen not so much as whiteness, as a matter of being true to one's essential nature.

Pure orange juice is devoid of additives . . . pure water is water and nothing else . . . a pure heart is a heart which is fully alive, with all its energies directed to a single end. . . . Purity of heart comes from being drawn toward God.

—Michael Casey
*The Undivided Heart: The Western
Monastic Approach to Contemplation*

When I feel lonely
ah, that's only a sign
some room is empty
that room is there by design
when I feel hollow
that's just my proof that there's more
for me to follow
that's what the lonely is for

—David Wilcox
"That's What the Lonely Is For"

Dan

As a young priest and monk, I was assigned to St. Scholastica in Detroit. While it wasn't part of my job description, one of my favorite things to do was play with the kids. It got to the point that the kids would come into the office and ask our stern, solemn-faced, but kind-hearted secretary, "Can Father Dan come out and play?"

Resonating her resignation to the situation, her voice would come over the intercom in my office: "Your little friends are here."

Sometimes the children asked if I had a wife and kids. It was not uncommon that when I said no, they would reply with a statement such as "Does that mean you love all of us the same?"

Celibacy is certainly a mixed bag, but it allows those of us who have chosen it as a way to God to learn how to love better. Religious celibates have given up the physical expression of sexuality, but we don't give up love. We are loved by and love many people. We are fully sexual human beings who are called to use our sexuality in life-giving ways.

Celibacy means curbing natural desires. Celibates aren't alone in learning to say no to sexual impulses.

Married people have to do the same if they're going to remain faithful to their vows. Celibacy allows the sexual impulse to be channeled into self-giving love. So does marriage. Just as monks learn lessons in love by practicing celibacy, married people learn about loving by loving one another and their family. Chastity isn't just for celibates.

When I play hockey, the men around me are not always aware that I'm a priest. So I've heard my share of locker-room talk. Many of the men frequently reduce women to derogatory labels and a list of body parts. Girlfriends and wives aren't excluded from the repulsive dehumanizing of women.

Much of what passes for love is actually lust. We see this impulse enshrined on movie screens and in music lyrics. Lust is a powerful drive, but it isn't love. The choice to love chastely is not an easy one. That's true whether one is married or a monastic.

Those same children I played with would often want their picture taken with me after their first communion or confirmation. On one occasion, someone's grandmother said to me, "Father, you must be in so many scrapbooks." That was one of the loneliest nights of my life.

Ultimately, no matter how we love or whom we love, we find ourselves alone. As songwriter Billy Joel sings, "You still wake up with yourself." The French talk about the sadness that comes after the loving.

This sadness is a witness to what we know is ultimately true, that there is a place inside every woman, man, and child that remains hungry for God. Even when you are completely known and intimately loved, it isn't enough to banish the loneliness every time. Every love, every impulse to love is actually about our craving for God. As David Wilcox writes, "That's what the lonely is for."

To love God singularly, as Benedict drives home, is to be true to what it means to genuinely love. The "pure in heart" we've all heard about are the people who have an unadulterated love for God. This doesn't mean they don't love people too. The loving of others flows from the love of God they experience.

Pure simply means that something is completely and only one thing. It is not mixed with anything else. It is not divided. We come to love God this way as we love one another reverently and selflessly. If we are not getting better at loving, we are missing the message of Jesus.

Going Inward

What do the terms *chaste, pure,* and *lonely* mean to you? Think about the times you have given and received genuine love. Did you find that true love was easy to recognize? Have you ever been treated as a commodity by someone who claimed to love you? How did it make you feel?

Spend some time thinking about what Benedict's words "Prefer nothing whatever to Christ" mean to you in a practical sense. How are you living this ideal?

Think about the assumptions we seldom question concerning the nature of love.

Holy One, I'm not sure I've ever loved anyone or anything with a whole heart. But there have been times when I have loved and I have known the joy of selflessness. There is a loneliness in me I can hardly name or bear to think about. It is not filled by all the best loves in my life or any of my best loving. Teach me to love, to be loved, and to recognize the call of the empty place in me that is reserved only for you. Amen.

6

HOSPITALITY

The Rule of St. Benedict

Let all guests who arrive be received like Christ, for he is going to say: *I was a stranger and you welcomed me* (Matt. 25:35). *And to all let due honor be shown, especially to those who share our faith* (Gal. 6:10) and to pilgrims. . . . In the reception of the poor and pilgrims the greatest care and solicitude should be shown, because it is especially in them that Christ is received.

—RB 53:1–2, 15

Other Voices

The threshold [of the doors we enter and leave from] comes to stand for the comings and goings of people throughout the days and years . . . the threshold prompts us to measure those comings and goings in a new way. Living is simple when the threshold is smooth enough for the innocent to cross and enter our lives and strong enough to bar the beguilers. God rightly frames the door to our souls and our lives as promised, and friend and neighbor freely cross its threshold.

—Martin Marty and Micah Marty
When True Simplicity Is Gained: Finding Spiritual Clarity in a Complex World

Once, we put up two white-robed young men who informed us that they were disciples of the Lord. The guest master offered to wash their robes made from bed sheets. One of the sheets was ripped to pieces in the washing machine, and Father Cletus had to provide the disciple with a new bed sheet. . . . We could have washed the feet of these pilgrims in white. Members of their group don't wear shoes. They walk from place to place barefoot. . . . We didn't wash their feet, though. Instead, Father Cletus showed the young men to the showers.

—Benet Tvedten
A Share in the Kingdom: A Commentary on the Rule of St. Benedict for Oblates

Lonni

I met Father Hilary the first time I attended Mass at St. Benedict Monastery. I have not seen him since. I enjoy a close and lasting friendship with the monks, but it would not have happened if not for Fr. Hilary. That bright summer morning also happened to be the celebration of the twenty-fifth anniversary of Fr. Dan's ordination.

I was waiting to go inside because I did not know how to get to the chapel. There were so many people, and I tend toward the shy side. A friend who knew more about the monastery than I did was supposed to meet me outside. So far, he was a no-show. After about fifteen minutes, I decided to leave.

Just as I was ready to dash for the parking lot, a slight, gray-haired monk with grace in his step began walking toward me. I had noticed him circling a few minutes before. My plan was to say good morning and get past him. But that morning I ran into one of the most gentle bulldozers I have ever encountered: Fr. Hilary. I've since heard that he's very shy.

He walked right up to me and introduced himself: "Father Hilary, like the president's wife, only nicer." He chuckled at his own joke. His English was broken by a strong Italian accent. He explained that he was from New Jersey and was visiting for Fr. Dan's celebration.

"You are a friend of Father Dan's?" he asked.

"Actually, I only met him recently."

"Well, it doesn't matter. It is a beautiful day to make new friends, eh?" He smiled with enough charm to open the gates of Fort Knox. I should have known then that the old darling had me in his sights and was moving in for the kill.

"You've read the Gospel of John?"

"Yes, I've read it."

"My favorite story is the one about the Samaritan woman—you like the story?"

I told him I liked it very much.

He chuckled, saying he had suspected so. Did I realize that not many people would know what story he meant? He didn't wait for an answer; instead he launched into his thoughts about the story. What did he like best? He was most struck by Jesus' excitement at meeting with and talking to this woman. Whatever had happened, Jesus was so thrilled that he couldn't eat afterward. It had been very meaningful to Jesus, this one conversation with a woman no one else would even talk to.

I don't know how he did it, but I was standing toe-to-toe with the silver-haired smoothy and he had my hand firmly clenched. There would be no escaping. We talked about the biblical story a little more; then he tucked my hand in the bend of his arm and started strolling toward the monastery door. His eyes twinkled. "Gotcha!"

"It is time for Mass now. I will take you to the chapel, but I cannot stay with you. You will see me in a few minutes, though," he said reassuringly. At the chapel entrance, I hesitated for the briefest moment. Fr. Hilary opened the door and smiled.

Benedictine hospitality at its best. He did what was not natural for him; he overcame his inherent shyness to reach out to me. Something about my discomfort compelled him to make me the object of his deepest graciousness.

Hospitality isn't about anything as simple as the best china, lace napkins, and crystal wineglasses. It might include those, but the real meaning of hospitality has to do with what one friend called "making room inside yourself for another person."

Going Inward

We often encounter opportunities to make room in our schedules, in ourselves, for another person. Yet the moment can come and go quickly. Consciously be aware when someone needs a moment of kindness, a little attention, a gracious gesture. Do this both at home and at work.

If hospitality means making room for another person, even in small ways, what could you do differently to become a more hospitable person?

Holy God, hospitality does not always come easily. There are so many other things to do, important things. I have responsibilities that get in the way of my best intentions. Give me eyes to see the possibilities and a heart big enough to make room for someone else. Amen.

7

HUMILITY

The Rule of St. Benedict

The first step of humility, then, is that we keep the fear of God always before our eyes and never forget it. We must constantly remember everything God has commanded . . . while guarding ourselves at every moment from sins and vices of thought or tongue, of hand or foot, of self-will or bodily desire. . . . The second step is that we come to love not our own will or our own pleasure. . . . The third step is that we submit in all obedience for the love of God.

—RB 7:10–12, 31, 34

Other Voices

What is humility? It is that habitual quality whereby we live in the truth of things: the truth that we are creatures and not the Creator; the truth that our life is a composite of good and evil, light and darkness; the truth that in our littleness we have been given extravagant dignity. . . . Humility is saying a radical "yes" to the human condition.

—Robert F. Morneau
Humility: 31 Reflections on Christian Virtue

Humility is a virtue, not a neurosis.

—Thomas Merton

Dan

Yes, we are dust, but we are also someone. A desert father is credited as saying that in life we need two stones. One says, "I am a worm"; the other says, "For me the universe was made." Remember both. That's humility.

One of the best cooks we've had at the monastery was Brother Ben. I recall telling him once that he made the best soup I had ever tasted, and he replied, "Father, when you tell me things like that, it's like water running off a duck's back." Then, as I turned away to leave, he said, "But the duck likes it."

In those few words, Br. Ben epitomized the essence of humility. It does not make a big deal out of personal abilities, talents, and so forth. It doesn't fuss about doing life and doing it well. However, it doesn't deny the pleasure in life well done either. It joyfully accepts affirmation without getting all puffed up about it.

St. Benedict got his ideas about humility from Jesus. "Do nothing from selfish ambition or conceit, but in humility regard others as better than yourselves. . . . Let the same mind be in you that was in Christ Jesus, who, though he was in the form of God, did not regard equality with God as something to be exploited, but emptied himself" (Phil. 2:3–7).

Benedict echoes this and tells us to regard others as superior to ourselves. Seem harsh? It's effective hyperbole because it rattles us. Jesus says to love others as you love yourself. That's easy. We don't blink at it anymore. But, when we're told to consider others superior, it exposes us. The state of our lukewarm love and our overinflated egos becomes piercingly clear. Jesus says that whoever wants to be first has to be last (see Mark 9:35), that we shouldn't try to get the best seat, and that we shouldn't try to impress others or be impressed too easily (see Luke 14:7–11).

During our youth retreats there is a time when we monks wash the feet of the teenagers. Our washing the feet of suddenly silent and nervously shifting teenagers is humility in action.

Where there are teens, you'll find noise, wall-buckling activity, and more than a touch of irreverence. But when we bend to the feet of the children, even the awkward giggles cease. An inviolable silence wraps around the assembly of teens and monks.

The service of the towel proclaims love in an unmistakable voice. Humility, at its best, bends before the lesser, the weaker, the younger, the older, the one who is not like me—not because of anything at all like self-degradation but because of the wonder of all humanity.

Humility is the opposite of humiliation. Humiliation denies the full dignity of humankind. Humility embraces the contradictions and glories of being human. We are the lost, we are the poor, and we are the weak. But we are also the found, the rich, and the strong.

Going Inward

Put someone before yourself today. Give up a seat on the bus; let someone else have the last piece of pie; surrender the best parking spot.

Write this prayer in your planner or post it somewhere in the house, and for the next few days pray it morning and evening:

Save me, God, from the distraction of trying to impress others. Save me also from the dangers of having done so. Help me to enjoy the praise I receive for a life well done. Help me to empty it gratefully into the ocean of your love. Teach me to learn from fair criticism, to hear it with a clear head, and to resist the urge to defend myself against it immediately. Give me good sense to remember that I'm not at the center of the universe. Free me from myself, my virtues, my powerful rightness. Lord, have mercy. Amen.

8

SERVICE

The Rule of St. Benedict

The brothers should serve one another. Consequently, no one will be excused from kitchen service unless he is sick or engaged in some important business of the monastery. Such service increases reward and fosters love. Let those who are not strong have help so that they may serve without distress.

—RB 35:1–3

Other Voices

A natural and understandable hesitancy accompanies any serious discussion of service. . . . We experience a fear that comes out something like this: "If I do that, people will take advantage of me, they will walk all over me."

Right here we must see the difference between choosing to serve and choosing to be a servant. When we choose to serve, we are still in charge. We decide whom we will serve and when we will serve. And if we are in charge, we will worry a great deal about anyone stepping on us, that is, taking charge over us.

But when we choose to be a servant, we give up the right to be in charge. There is great freedom in this. If we voluntarily choose to be taken advantage of, then we cannot be manipulated. When we choose to be a servant, we surrender the right to decide who and when we will serve. We become available and vulnerable.

—Richard Foster
Celebration of Discipline:
The Path to Spiritual Growth

Dan

For many years we've hosted a special week when youth and adults get together and spend the week serving others. We call it Project People. It's the brainchild of Mary Cummings, who has worked with me in youth ministry since my days as a young monk and priest.

One year, we took a crew of teens to a home that was overgrown with brush and saplings. Usually, we look a job over before tackling it, but in this case, we had not been able to make it to the job site in advance. We expected an average overabundant lawn. Words fail to describe the gnarled, tall thicket we encountered.

One of our rules is that the kids can't use motorized tools. After seeing the colossal job ahead, we resolved ourselves to the work, and I began unloading unmotorized tools that suddenly looked about as effective as butter knives. Rich, a ninth-grade boy, took a sweeping look at the dense jungle and said, "But, Father Dan, we're just kids."

The homeowner was an endearing, sweet, elderly woman who, because of her health, rarely left her home. During the week, we got to know this wonderful woman and were amazed at her cheerfulness even though she lived with physical limits that kept her from ever going very far out of her house. The kids covered the back window so that she would not see our day-to-day progress. Instead, when the work was finished, she would have the delight of seeing the transformation in its entirety.

Every day a couple of the teens would go inside to share our sandwiches with her. They often came out in tears, moved by her positive attitude despite what had been a very difficult life.

By the end of the week everyone was feeling good about all we'd accomplished and the delight the woman experienced in our presence. Finally the long, hard work was finished. Her absolute pleasure in seeing the transformed backyard gave the teens an unforgettable moment. Rich told me later that he had never realized the joy that comes from helping others. He isn't the only kid, or adult, who has said something like that after a week of Project People.

Look around—there are countless little ways to serve one another. There is the service of listening. Counselors tell us that there's hardly a person they counsel who has any need except for someone to listen to them. Simple helpfulness and common courtesy are easy ways to serve every day of our lives.

Like Rich, we sometimes feel intimidated by circumstances. The job can appear overwhelming and our tools limited. If we press beyond the thing that seems to limit, we will astound ourselves with our own capacity to serve and the joy it gives.

Going Inward

Pay close attention today for opportunities to serve others in subtle ways. Get someone's coffee; wash another's car; make a sandwich. Think about how you felt when you made a conscious effort to serve others. There are probably many ways you already serve your family, friends, and neighbors.

How are self-giving service and simply helping out the same? How are they different? What is your experience of both?

Every day this week, look for some little service you can give someone. Write in your journal about the ways you would like to serve others and how your own experience compares to the ideal of self-giving service.

Contact your parish, school, or a service group about an opportunity to make a special effort in service of others. Most communities have soup kitchens, youth centers, shelters for battered women and children, street missions, and so forth. Set aside time to do something special.

Servant God, there's an awful lot to do, you know. A person could get overwhelmed and intimidated by the sheer magnitude of all the good causes and all the hurting, needy people. Still, there must be something I can do, something that my experience and talents will lend themselves to. Make my heart open to others. Give me sight to see the needs and strength of joy to persevere in the work of loving and serving. Remind me that I don't have to do it all. I only have to do my share. Amen.

9

LEARNING

The Rule of St. Benedict

Therefore we intend to establish a school for the Lord's service.

RB Prologue:45

Other Voices

It cannot be that people should grow in grace unless they give themselves to reading. A reading people will always be a knowing people. A people who talk much will know little. . . . You can never be deep . . . without [reading] . . . fix some part of every day for private exercises. . . . Whether you like it or not, read and pray daily. It is your life; there is no other way; else you will be a trifler all your days.

—John Wesley
Quoted in *The Message of the Wesleys*

Benedictines are traditionally identified with scholarship as well as liturgy. This stereotype is only partly accurate . . . part of the impetus was entirely pragmatic: Benedictines (of St. Benedict's era) had to be taught how to read and what to read. The literacy of newcomers to the monastery could by no means be presumed . . . the sources from which Benedict drew in writing his Rule display an ambivalence toward learning that runs throughout western monastic history. Early monastic writers protest the dangers of study for its own sake. . . . None the less, the copying of manuscripts and the composition of original works of theology, biblical commentary or natural science developed naturally from Benedict's emphasis on Lectio. Inevitably, some found themselves drawn more and more deeply into the texts they read, and were inspired to contribute to the tradition they had received.

—Columba Stewart, o.s.b.
Prayer and Community: The Benedictine Tradition

Lonni

Jean Leclercq, o.s.b., titled his book about monastic culture *The Love of Learning and the Desire for God.* A teachable spirit indicates that present in the human heart are some important elements for spiritual growth. It demonstrates that we don't think we know it all. It exposes us to thoughts that are new and not our own.

Additionally, learning reveals our desires, the deepest hungers we have. For all these reasons, Leclercq links the desire for learning and the desire for God.

When someone enters a monastery, there is a lengthy period in which he is a novice. He takes classes, he learns to pray, he learns to seek God, he learns how to live in community, and he learns the basics of becoming a monk. It's understood in monasteries that the spiritual journey involves learning. So the journey begins with what could be considered a rather humble role—the state of novice, wet-behind-the-ears beginner. The man who can't admit that he's got a lot to learn will have little affinity for monastic life.

Brother John-Martin was a novice at St. Benedict's the day he and I worked together sanding, staining, and varnishing boards for the ceiling of the new chapel. John-Martin is the most analytical person I've ever met. When you input data (speak to him) you can actually watch him process the data (think) before he responds (replies). It's fascinating and quite endearing as well.

That was my third or fourth weekend working on boards along with other friends of the community. Novice John-Martin was also a novice at the process of finishing ceiling boards.

I was sanding. Br. John-Martin stood only a few inches away from me with a can of stain and a paint-brush. He asked if someone could explain the process—what were we doing, why were we doing it, and what the steps were. His tone of voice was the same as if he had just asked us to explain quantum physics to him.

It simply wasn't that difficult. I glanced up from my work, power sander in hand, and smiled. "John-Martin, just put the brush on the board." Brother Damien grinned and said, "Never argue with a woman holding a power tool."

There was a fifteen-second-or-so pause from the man beside me. Then he dipped his brush in the can of stain and said triumphantly, "Brush on board—I can do that!"

John-Martin is a learner. He is willing to try. He can get past his passion for detail and put his hand to the task before him. He immediately recognized that the task was within his abilities and, even though it was a new experience, he could learn to do it. He will learn all of his life, and his learning will take him to God.

Novices aren't the only ones with a lot to learn. A lifetime is hardly enough time to contain all there is to discover in our world. Not long ago I was speaking with a monk who is much older than Br. John-Martin. He had undergone surgery, followed by weeks of pain. Father Thomas admitted that while suffering is certainly a way to God, it is also not easy. "We are all not very good at it," he said, shaking his head. "We are all just learning."

Going Inward

With the vast amount of knowledge that is still ours to acquire, we hardly know where to begin. Select a book that has been recommended to you by someone you trust (or pick one from the suggested reading list in the back of this book). Scan the book your first time through, gathering as much information as you can. Then read it again, very slowly. The third time through it, underline whatever you want and write in the margins.

Begin a notebook in which you outline and keep notes on all your reading. In the back of this notebook, or somewhere convenient, keep a list of books you'd like to read.

On a "teachable" scale are you average, above average, or below average? What prevents you from learning more? What encourages you to learn?

God, grant to me a teachable spirit, a mind wide with possibilities and eager to embrace knowledge. Make me hungry to learn and humble enough to enjoy it. I do not yet know it all. Don't let me forget that. Amen.

10

REVERENCE

The Rule of St. Benedict

Let the tools of the monastery and its whole property be regarded as if they were the sacred vessels of the altar.

—RB 31:10

Allow no one to treat the monastery's tools and implements in a slovenly or careless way.

—RB 32:4

Other Voices

That's the thing about Benedict . . . he says what hardly anyone else has ever said, that the things we touch (and the people we touch) are to be touched reverently. We're a tool-making people, even our highest technologies are simply complicated tools. The tools are our own creation; the tools make possible the act of creating. But there's this love-hate thing that goes on between us and our tools. Benedict knows that when we begin to accept and treat gently our tools, we will begin to accept and treat gently ourselves and others.

We want to be free of this tool-making drive. We want to escape our basic genuine self that likes to tinker, likes to polish floors and likes to mow the lawn. How demeaning, we think. In a day and age when we can pay someone else to do anything for us, or we can turn a switch and a machine will do it, what are educated, aware, and gosh-darn important people thinking when they bake bread or trim the hedge? And what are they smiling about while they're working?

Could it be that those who smile that smile do so because they have found the pleasure of reverence when there's a tool in their hand? They have learned to sense something bigger and holier and better in the tools of their life. To handle carefully what we hold in our hand, is to come to terms with ourselves. It is to accept ourselves. When I pick up the rake, or the wooden bowl, or when I turn a faucet, I am entering into my place in creation. We are absolutely nothing in the bigger scheme. There's a lot of liberty in not being so important. At the same time, we discover by our tools that we might be only a molecule in the plan of a vast Creation, but we are a spectacular molecule set spinning by the hand of God, and our presence is miraculous.

—Lonni Collins Pratt
"Reverence: The Untried Path"
Christian Living Magazine

Lonni

I've noticed it myself, and Father Dan tells me others have commented on the way Brother Antony butters toast. He usually prepares toast for the retreat kids' big breakfast. He once buttered a piece of toast for me at the community breakfast table while I was visiting. He carefully covers the entire slice of toast, taking his time and paying attention to what he does. He does the same thing if he's setting a table, painting a room, or sanding a board. When Fr. Dan mentioned to him that others had commented on how attentively he prepares toast, Br. Antony said, "I just do each one as if it were my own."

As a college student, I worked part of a summer in a Missouri women's shelter. That's where I met Sister Becca. I think her name was Rebecca, but we called her Sr. Becca. I don't know if she was a Benedictine. I was young and not noticing such things. And I was so full of the "important" work I did that I hardly ever took time to talk to this middle-aged (I thought), tall nun with lines in her face and steel in laughing dark eyes.

But I did notice this: At the beginning of every workday, the utensils needed to prepare breakfast were laid out on the large butcher-block counter in the kitchen.

They were placed carefully, in the order we would use them. Dish towels were put within easy reach. The food items we would need were at the front of the refrigerator. The menu and recipes were placed in wall-mounted plastic sleeves over the stoves.

One day, Sr. Becca walked into the kitchen about 6:30 A.M. I was working alone, and I was frantic. My kitchen partner was back at our room sleeping off a bad flu bug she had caught from the shelter's children. I was up to my elbows in pancake batter. My hair had escaped from the clip that kept it secured at the back of my head, and it was flying around my face and shoulders (and into the batter).

Sr. Becca said good morning, lifted my hair from my shoulders, reclipped it with motherly tenderness, then picked up an apron and asked what she could do. For the next couple of hours we worked and talked. Sr. Becca was the founder of the shelter. She was retired and much older than she appeared. She had severe arthritis, but she liked to "help out now and then" at the shelter. One of the "little things" she did was lay out our work implements before going to bed. I learned later that she did the same thing for the workers in the laundry room and nursery.

After that, when I entered the large kitchen at 5:30 A.M. and saw the kitchen tools laid out so reverently, with all the thought Sr. Becca had put into our needs, it would slow me down for a minute. It became a holy pause in my day. I could never pick up the tools without seeing her long, gnarled hands laying them down with purposeful care. I would remember that she had thought of us, of me, in those last hours of the day. When I stirred with the old wooden spoon or fried eggs in the huge cast-iron fry pan or mixed batter in the slightly chipped, very deep pottery bowl, I employed Sr. Becca's prayer. The tools of the kitchen became prayers clutched in my hand.

In the same way, the care Br. Antony takes with each slice of toast is prayer for each young adult who will eat the toast. It is not a simple task; it is ardent intercessory employment.

Going Inward

As you pick up the tools of your work today, be aware of how they feel in your hand. Consider the kind of work you do, who it affects, and what it does for you and your family.

Pick two or three tools you use and take time to pray with each in your hand. Pray for the work you do. Pray for those who benefit from the work.

Is your own attitude one of reverence for the many good things in your life that enable you to create and give?

Write out the prayers you prayed and use them for the next month whenever you use the same tool.

God, with the tools I hold in my hand, empower me to do your work. The tools of our labor are holy vessels by which the kingdom of God comes among us. When I reverence the tools of my work, I reverence myself, and I give myself worth and value. There are plenty of people who will try to rip away portions of my self-worth. When I hold my tools, remind me that I matter and that the work matters. Amen.

11

POSSESSIONS

The Rule of St. Benedict

Above all, this poisoning practice, possessing, must be uprooted and removed from the monastery. We insist that without the abbot's permission, no one may presume to give, accept, or keep anything as personal property. . . . *All things should be the common possession of all . . . so that no one* presumes *to call anything his own* (Acts 4:32).

—*RB 33:1–3, 6*

Other Voices

We have been brainwashed to believe that bigger houses, more prosperous businesses, more luxurious gadgets, are worthy goals in life. As a result, we are caught in an absurd, materialistic spiral. The more we make, the more we think we need in order to live decently and respectably. Somehow we have to break this cycle because it makes us sin against our needy brothers and sisters and, therefore, against our Lord. And it also destroys us. Sharing with others is the way to real joy.

—Ron Sider
Rich Christians in an Age of Hunger

Their property held them in chains . . . which shackled their courage and choked their faith . . . and throttled their souls. . . . They think of themselves as owners, whereas it is they rather who are owned; enslaved as they are to their own property.

—Cyprian, third-century bishop of Carthage

. . . the rich man . . . who held his things lightly and who did not let them nestle in his heart, who was a channel and not a cistern, who was ever and always forsaking his money—this rich man starts (in heaven) side by side with the man who accepted, not hated, his poverty. Each will say, "I am free."

—George MacDonald

Lonni

The department-store commercial opens with shots of all things being prepared for students to return to school after summer vacation. The buses are ready. The halls are shining. The boards have been washed and the bells set. Switch scenes to a young adolescent girl in her bedroom. She realizes it's back-to-school time, and she cries out, aghast, "Mom, I have nothing to wear!" Behind her is a closet jammed tight, erupting at the hinges with clothing. She couldn't fit a T-shirt in there. What she meant was she didn't have anything "cool."

We shake our heads at the girl and wonder at the materialistic teen culture. But as adults, are we really so different? Ours is a supersized culture. You want a burger and a soda? Well, just try to get through a fast-food place without some eager employee urging you to supersize. Get more, have more, consume more—that's what we are continually pushed to do. We have lost a sense of enough.

Benedict is pretty hard on any monk who would dare to utter the words, "I own." His attitude is radically different from the unspoken statement of success we are taught all our lives: "I own; therefore I am."

Benedict wants his monks to have enough. Even a quick review of the Rule reveals that he is a practical man who understands that people have needs and who is concerned about providing for the needs of his monks. They should have enough clothing, a bed of their own, abundant food, shelter, and whatever tools they require for their work. Benedict doesn't expect anyone to do without the essentials. But he understands that the act of owning sets us up, if we aren't careful, to believe a lie.

Owning sets us up for a fall because it imparts a false sense of security. After all, ownership is not the same as ultimate control. Our white-knuckled grip on possessions won't keep away wind, fire, and economic disaster. Uninvited birds will land in the tree we own as if the thing belongs to them. Furniture, clothing, and cars will break, wear out, and crash.

Benedict says to give it up, forget about it. That doesn't mean we shouldn't have houses or property or cars or shoes. It means that we shouldn't attach ourselves to things. That's not what things are for.

When building a spectacular new chapel, the monks of St. Benedict Monastery chose to reuse items from the old chapel, such as their crucifix and altar, rather than purchasing everything new.

One of the monks, Father Mike Green, wears a coat that has seen many a winter. It isn't fashionable—actually it could hardly be called presentable—but it is still usable. It keeps him warm; it still fits him. Why would he toss it out for a new one?

When I watch Fr. Mike rumble across the snowy hills of the monastery atop his tractor, bundled into his coat, I stand reminded that ownership isn't important for happiness. It's an important witness of monasticism

in an era in which we are bludgeoned with advertise-
ments insisting that we need more, we have a right to
it, we deserve it, it will make us happier, sexier, and
younger—so get out there and buy it.

Monks intentionally surrender certain options most
of us take for granted. Ownership is one of those
options. Benedict's Rule calls the monk to the "path of
life." The path of life, as Benedict presents it, calls us
away from the jungles of consumption and possession
and into freedom.

Going Inward

For the next month, place yourself under a moratorium
on shopping (except for groceries). Find ways to use
what you already have. Consider how owning and buying might be feeding your ego. Why is it important to
have the newest clothes or the newest technology?

When you bring something new into your home,
give something away.

Consider your relationship to ownership. Do you
find yourself defending your right to own? Are there
times when you have wondered if your possessing and
spending are out of control?

There is such a thing as responsible ownership—if we "hold lightly" what we own. What do you think that means? Talk to someone you trust about it.

Spend half a day alone considering ways you can pare down the amount of stuff you possess.

Lord of the enough, help me to understand moderation not as self-denial but as the celebration of all that I already possess. It's hard to resist the cultural voices compelling me to spend and accumulate. Help me focus on the abundance around me. Teach me to be grateful. Teach me to enjoy what I have. Teach me to know when enough is enough. Amen.

12

RESPONSIBILITY

The Rule of St. Benedict

If the community is rather large, a few brothers should be chosen on account of their good reputations and holy life, and they should be made deans. They will take care of their groups of ten, managing all affairs according to the commandments of God and the orders of their abbot.

—RB 21:1–2

At the door of the monastery, place a sensible old man who knows how to take a message and deliver a reply.

—RB 66:1

A brother may be assigned a difficult task or something he cannot do. If this happens, he should, with utter gentleness and obedience, accept the order he is given. Should he see that the weight of the burden is altogether unreasonable, he should look for the proper moment and explain patiently to his superior the reasons he cannot perform the task. This he ought to do without pride. . . . If after the explanation, the superior is still determined to hold to his original order, then the junior must recognize that this is best for him. Trusting in God's help, he must, in love, obey.

—*RB 68:1–5*

Other Voices

Accountability and responsibility—these two words express crucial aspects of being human. No man is an island. We are a part of all whom we have met. . . . Once we recognize accountability we will accept responsibility to order our lives in a manner which will execute decisions consistent with our roles. Our conscience will not let us play games . . .

—Myron Augsburger
The Christ-Shaped Conscience

Dan

B rother Benedict is our cow man. He has faithfully tended our herd for forty years—even though he was in his mid-forties, with no cattle experience, when he began.

Once, at 1 A.M., in the middle of a youth retreat I encountered Br. Ben on his way to the barn, expecting a calf to be born. Finding him again an hour later, I asked how it went. "She says no," he replied. When I expressed regret that the blessed event had not occurred despite his middle-of-the-night efforts, he grinned and said, "Well, that's the life of a cowboy!"

Br. Ben takes the birth of a calf seriously. The mother is pampered while awaiting her little one's arrival. When a cow is close to delivering, Br. Ben always makes sure she is in the barn. He feels a strong sense of responsibility for the cow and calf.

It was because he couldn't get a particularly stubborn cow into the barn that Br. Ben woke up Father Mike and me in the middle hours of the night. She was about to deliver, she was in the pasture, and he wanted her in the barn. He was racked with anxiety about the birth.

We tried to convince him that cows deliver out in fields all the time and she would be fine. Our sleepy reassurances didn't ease his mind, so we ended up in the pasture chasing an about-to-deliver cow that didn't want to go into the barn.

I managed to get a rope around her, but the grass was wet with dew and I ended up water-skiing behind her across the field. Br. Ben continued to worry. The cow got away. I roped her again and once more went skimming across the wet grass. Only this time she pulled me up a slope, and I did a complete 360-degree flip, flashlight and all—and guess what I landed in? The Bible calls it dung. By this time Fr. Mike and I were *really* ready to give up. Br. Ben would hear none of it (sometimes his deafness comes in handy!).

So, there stood the cow. She was in dust rather than grass, not far from the fence. We convinced Br. Ben it would be OK if we tied her to the fence for the delivery. Moments later, with the help of chains and our midwifery skills, a fresh, wet calf was delivered with a thump into the dust. The poor little thing came up with dust in its eyes, trying to breathe while inhaling the grime, and being otherwise pathetic.

By now Mike and I really cared about this calf. But Br. Ben understood the limits of his responsibility. "I'm going to bed. We've done all we can. God bless you," he announced. He thanked us and walked away while we stood waiting for whatever happened next. He was right; there was nothing left to be done. It was a good time to go to bed.

Br. Ben, who always takes his responsibilities to heart, knows when it's over. But Fr. Mike and I were involved by now. We had a calf, and the cowboy was going to bed, leaving us there in the pasture, feeling responsible with nothing to do.

Responsibility is a recurrent theme in the Rule of St. Benedict. Benedict expects that his monks will take seriously whatever they put their hands to. All of us have responsibilities. Accepting this reality and embracing it is a sign of maturity. It's a vital lesson. But we have to learn to recognize when we've done all we can.

Contemporary people go to extremes on this. There is the personality that overworks, overcommits, and never delegates, and then there's the personality that never quite accepts responsibility. Both approaches are to be avoided.

As the oldest child in a big family, I learned early how to be responsible. Like with many firstborn children, it just seemed to come naturally to me—sometimes to an extreme. The importance of accepting responsibility can't be overemphasized. Just as important, though, is knowing when to let go, knowing when we've done all that is in our power. Responsible living means embracing both realities.

Going Inward

Which responsibilities do you take most seriously? Which ones are the hardest for you?

Pay attention to the messages you receive about responsibility from the media and the people around you. What are the prevalent messages?

To be responsible is to be given a trust by God to care for something or someone. How would attitudes toward responsibility change if we thought of it in this manner? What can you do to make your responsibilities more joyful?

Is your attitude toward responsibility realistic? Do you know the limits? Talk to someone close to you about it. Ask if you seem to handle responsibility appropriately.

Father, it's not easy to be clear about what I'm responsible for and when it's time to let go. I want to control, yet I want to escape personal responsibility. Show me where and when I go to extremes. Amen.

13

REASONABLE
BALANCE

The Rule of St. Benedict

In establishing the monastery regulations, we hope to set down nothing harsh and nothing burdensome. The good of all concerned prompts us to a little strictness in order to rectify faults and to safeguard love.

—RB Prologue:46–47

There ought to be an appropriate proportion between the seriousness of a fault and the measure of discipline.

—RB 24:1

The abbot should regulate and arrange all things so that souls might be saved and the monks may go about their activities without justifiable grumbling.

—RB 41:5

Other Voices

Can you, from time to time, just nurture a little warm feeling toward yourself? I truly believe that's all it takes (for sanity and realistic expectations). A little warm feeling creates an atmosphere of acceptance, of allowing, of permitting. And within that atmosphere there is a kind of encouragement for the goodness to grow: the goodness that is you, the goodness that is life in you, the goodness of creation in you, God's goodness in you.

—Gerald May
Simply Sane

Lonni

One of the most outstanding traits of the Rule is how reasonable it is. Compared with other rules of the period, it is concise, lucid, and realistic. There are no long lists of details about diet, garb, or behavior. It is bare-bones sanity. It is what I find most compelling about the Rule. The result is a balanced and kind way to live. Benedict suggests nothing harsh. By being reasonable, we can avoid the extremes that burn us out and leave us sleepless.

Benedict is starkly sensible. Benedictines, as a result of living with the Rule, end up being delightfully sensible people living simple and balanced lives. They find time for play as well as prayer. They hold to the standards of the church without ever judging others. Their lives of reasonable balance are excellent examples.

A few years ago, a group of novices at the monastery were given the task of painting the novitiate (the residence of the novices). They were a lively group of guys who were as capable of mischief as any group of young men I've ever known. They did not simply paint. They emblazoned the name of each monk on the side of the novitiate with some comment, a pun, a joke, or a nickname. It was good-natured, harmless fun. The next day, they painted over it and finished the job of sprucing up the building.

Over dinner that evening, I watched the faces of the older monks as they listened to the novices talk about what they had done. There was a lot of laughter, but a couple of the monks looked a bit concerned about the playful streak in their novices.

The one man who had it within his power to make those young men regret their spontaneous fun, Father Dan, their prior, appeared to enjoy their antics more than any of the others. He clearly did not expect them to stop being young or to set aside all shenanigans now that they were Benedictine novices.

His understanding of human nature is insightful and realistic. I've noticed it with how he handles the teens on retreats also. For example, the kids go to bed late, sleep in, and have breakfast at 10:00 or 10:30. Why put everyone through the stress of trying to get the kids into bed early and up for breakfast early?

Fr. Dan is good at being reasonable, but he is also capable of holding the line when the issue is an important one. Like Benedict, he knows that at times you have to take a stand. The trick is knowing when the situation calls for the "strictness" Benedict mentions and when it's reasonable to be gentle in the way Gerald May mentions.

In our own age, there are a lot of unreasonable expectations crowding us. Benedict still leads us away from the more complicated paths bogged down in legalism and unrealistic expectations and into a path of gentle sanity. We hear the echo of Jesus in Benedict's words, telling us that his burden is light and his yoke is easy. Listen, all you who are tired, pushed around, and uptight. You'll find rest.

Going Inward

Identify the ways you are unreasonable with yourself and with others. Are your expectations of God reasonable? Remember a time when an unrealistic expectation led to complications. What could have been done to change the situation?

Jesus, you always expected the best of others, but you never tried to make them into something they weren't. You were gentle and strong, reasonable at all times, even though others didn't always understand. I want to accept myself, others, and the life I am given with realistic expectations. Teach me gentle sanity, quiet delight in God, myself, and others. Amen.

14

CONVERSION
OF LIFE

The Rule of St. Benedict

Yearn for everlasting life with holy desire. Day by day remind yourself that you are going to die. Hour by hour keep careful watch over all you do, aware that God's gaze is upon you, wherever you may be.

—RB 4:46–49

Do not aspire to be called holy before you really are, but first be holy that you may more truly be called so.

—RB 4:62

It is love that impels them to pursue everlasting life; therefore, they are eager to take the narrow road. . . .They no longer live by their own judgment, giving in to their whims and appetites.

—RB 5:10–12

Other Voices

It took the hand of God Almighty
to part the waters in the sea
But it only took one little lie

to separate you and me
Oh we are not as strong as we think we are.

We are frail
We are fearfully and wonderfully made
Forged in the fire of human passion
Choking on the fumes of selfish rage
And with these our hells and our heavens
So few inches apart
We must be awful small
And not as strong as we think we are.

When you love you walk on the water
Just don't stumble on the waves
We all want to go there somethin' awful
But to stand there it takes some grace
Cause we are not as strong as we think we are.

—Rich Mullins and Beaker
"We Are Not as Strong as We Think We Are"

Lonni and Dan

John Mellencamp's grandfather died the day after Christmas in 1983. John was shaken by the sight of his usually stoic German Lutheran grandfather terrified by death and paralyzed by a "rustic pride that prevented him from acknowledging his own fear of the devil or his faith in redemption."

Standing beside his dying grandfather, Mellencamp had a moment of conversion. His grandfather had had a long lifetime to accept the reality of death. Mellencamp was struck with how little this man he loved and respected had prepared himself for his final moments. Benedict teaches that an awareness of death will convert us. It will keep us honest. It will keep us trying.

We all avoid the tough issues. We are not as strong or as good as we want to be or think we are. Conversion moments take us one step closer to the goal. Some have called them "aha" moments. It's when something shatters and something shines and we know something for the first time but are sure we've known it all along. We're different after a moment like that. We know there's no going back to who we were a moment before. In some sense, conversion is a dying moment.

As a result of Mellencamp's conversion moment he wrote "Paper in Fire." It gathers up his feelings about life and death, family, and faith. It's about dreams burned up, love without involvement, the days of vanity that pass quickly. We each see our "days burn up like paper in fire," wrote Mellencamp.

In "Paper in Fire," John Mellencamp paraphrased Benedict's words: "Remind yourself that you are going to die . . . keep careful watch over all you do." It's no doomsday attitude either writer is suggesting, but a realistic view of the world and of ourselves.

Monks vow themselves to conversion of life. They promise that whatever happens, they will keep themselves on the hard course of becoming more authentically human. That's conversion. Shut the door to yesterday and start over, every single day of your life.

"Going to work on Monday / got yourself a family / all the bills have been paid / Can't tell your best buddy that you love him / where does our time go / that brand new house in escrow / sleep with your back to the one you love the most / and it's all that we've learned about happiness . . . forgot to say hello to my neighbor, sometimes I question my own religion . . .

and this is all that we've learned about living," wrote Mellencamp in another song, "Check It Out."

Conversion involves a continual turning to God. Benedict knew that a good place to begin is with severe honesty. We only get so many days. Remember that. Throw your whole self into living the present moment. Live and love so that you won't have any regrets.

Going Inward

What if today were your last day?

We've heard it so much that it sounds trite. One author I know bought his own cemetery plot and spent a couple weeks of his vacation sitting in a lawn chair on the site. It changed his life. Imagine yourself in that chair.

The power of conversion is invested in the sense of our mortality. It slaps us with the question we've reduced to shallow meaninglessness rather than face like grown-ups. You're going to die, Benedict bellows. So what are you going to do with your life?

God, conversion is a pretty scary word. I don't understand how it happens or what is expected of me. But I need to make changes that I can't seem to make on my own. You will have to change me. Make me more

aware of how you're doing that and how I can cooper-
ate with you. Remind me to begin again, no matter
how often I get sidetracked or lose my way. Remind me
I can't do it alone. I will always need you. Amen.

15

CONFLICT

The Rule of *St. Benedict*

For certain, Lauds and Vespers must never conclude without the superior's reciting the entire Lord's Prayer at the end for everyone to hear, because thorns of discord are likely to spring up. Therein warned by the pledge they make to one another in this prayer: *Forgive us as we forgive* (Matt. 6:12), they may rid themselves of this failing.

—*RB 13:12–13*

As administrator of the monastery, there should be chosen . . . someone who is wise. . . . He will take care of everything, but will do nothing without an order from the abbot. . . . He should not annoy his brothers. If any brother happens to make an unreasonable demand of him, he should not reject him with disdain and cause him distress, but reasonably and humbly deny the improper request.

—*RB 31:1–7*

Respect the elders and love the young. . . . If you have a disagreement with someone, make peace with them before the sun goes down. Finally, and importantly, never lose hope in God's mercy.

—RB 4:70–74

Other Voices

Why are some people thrown off by irritations while others remain lighthearted about them? Why do some stagger under the burden of duty, while others carry it lightly? A complainer asks, "Why am I on some days done in by the drudgeries while on others I am able to laugh at a long and hopelessly demanding agenda?" . . . The lesson is clear: if the spirit with which we greet the day's details is serene, the challenges of the day will not be daunting. Rather than paste on an artificial smile and grimly set about our work, we learn to laugh defiantly when the lists and agendas are long—and to keep a perspective that allows a blitheness to develop and to color the actions of the day.

—Martin Marty and Micah Marty
When True Simplicity Is Gained: Finding Spiritual Clarity in a Complex World

Lonni

The monk who told me about his prior's "easy forgiveness" looked surprised when he told me the story. It was a hectic time for the monk. He was a middle-aged man cramming for midterms at school. It was the anniversary of one of his deepest tragedies. His brother and family were in the midst of a crisis. The monk had lost control of his anger and erupted, putting into writing all his complaints—and most were, he admitted, petty.

He then shoved the letter under the prior's door and for a little while felt much better.

However, the satisfaction didn't last long. By morning he regretted his hasty blowup and regretted even more that his prior had the evidence in his hand.

"After morning prayer I asked him if I could speak to him. He said he had appointments all morning, 'but we'll discuss this later.' Then he put his hand on my shoulder and said, 'Don't worry. You're forgiven.'"

The praying of the Lord's Prayer at least twice a day is St. Benedict's remedy for conflict. At the root is the concept of forgiveness. It isn't always necessary to address every offense. Sometimes, it's OK to overlook the offense and just move on. Our motivations for wanting confrontation are not always pure. Sometimes it's the attention, or the satisfaction of being right, we're actually craving.

There are situations in which confrontation is the only reasonable response to conflict. Every offense cannot be overlooked. But even in those most serious situations, the Christian ideal is eventual forgiveness. This may or may not make possible a relationship with the offender, but it frees the one who forgives to move past the pain.

Benedict knows that people who live together are going to grind against one another. People in intimate relationships will get on each other's nerves. For many of these problems, the simple answer is to understand and forgive.

Going Inward

Pay close attention to the little moments of grace that are extended to you by others today. Look for opportunities to do the same. Don't flash your headlights or pound the horn when someone pulls in front of you. Let someone in line before you. Be patient with the person who is short-tempered. Cultivate a forgiving attitude for the lapses of the people you work with and live with. Before going to sleep tonight, think about the opportunities you had to forgive and the times others were called upon to forgive you. Pray the Lord's Prayer before falling asleep.

Our Father in heaven, forgive my sins as I forgive those who sin against me, who sin against all of us. Wipe up the messes we make, and don't let me get so full of myself that I forget that I've contributed to the mess. Teach me to forgive. Remind me that I need to be forgiven. Lord, have mercy. Amen.

16

FRIENDSHIP

The Rule of St. Benedict

All guests who present themselves are to be welcome as Christ.

—*RB 53:1*

To their fellow monks they show the pure love of brothers.

—*RB 72:8*

Other Voices

Vowing to stay in one place with the same people for the rest of our life is a commitment to appreciate unending beauty in the simplest elements . . . every one of his [the monk's] brothers was brought to this place by God. Their presence . . . is sacramental.

—Frank Bianco
Voices of Silence: Lives of the Trappists Today

[Frank Bianco, the author, notes that the cemetery at New Melleray has only about one hundred crosses, although a plaque indicated that some two hundred and fifty monks had died. He asks the abbot, Dom Jacques, "Where are the missing monks?"]

"Missing? No, all of our monks are there. No one is missing." It would not do, he explained, to have the cemetery growing endlessly. If a monk died, they would open up the oldest grave, gather any bones that remained, put them in a cardboard box and position the box beneath the head of the monk who was to be buried.

"So, the dead monk becomes his brother's pillow," I suggested.

"Pillow?" Dom Jacques asked, reaching for his (French-English) dictionary. "Pillow, pillow," he repeated. . . . "Ah, yes, *Oreiller*—pillow. That's right," he said, grinning. . . . "Pillow. When I die, my brother who never knew me, will be my . . . pillow, and eventually we will both be the pillow for a monk neither of us ever knew."

—Frank Bianco
Voices of Silence: Lives of the Trappists Today

Lonni

Over the weekend my husband and I had hosted a cookout for our nineteen-year-old daughter and her groom. They had eloped to Toledo. I had grave doubts about the marriage, about their future, and about myself as a parent. But we threw the party, we held them close, and we hoped with all our energy for all the best for them.

The next day, I took a case of beer, baked beans, and two dozen submarine sandwiches to the monastery. I figured the party surplus was the kind of guy food the monks would enjoy. No one was around when I arrived. So much the better; I could stuff the stuff in their refrigerator and be gone. I didn't want to explain to anyone how I had failed my child, thereby causing her to run away to Toledo.

Before I could unload the boxes, Brother Ben entered the kitchen door, fresh from the barn. He greeted me with open arms, told me about some pesky raccoons, then motioned quizzically toward the subs and beer.

"For the retreat house? Do you need help?" he asked. If so, he would help.

"No, it's not for the retreat house; it's for you," I said. I explained about the party and my daughter in a few restrained, unemotional sentences. Because of his poor hearing, he probably only caught about half of what I was saying. I'm sure the look on my face told all.

Br. Ben nodded, he smiled even wider, and he motioned again to the boxes. "All for me?" he asked with a light in his eyes.

"I think you should share with your brothers," I replied in a very maternal tone.

He laughed, swatted the top of my head lightly with his newspaper, squeezed my hand, then offered me coffee. Nothing was different. But I felt better. In his way, Br. Ben had just said, "It will be OK. And if it isn't, you will be OK anyway. Whatever happens, you have me."

I remembered Father Dan telling me a story about Br. Ben that sounded similar. Fr. Dan had been preoccupied during prayer but wasn't aware that his countenance revealed the concerns he carried. After prayer, Br. Ben said, "You look like you lost your last friend."

Then the older monk looked into the eyes of the much younger prior, the boy he had watched become a man, a monk, and eventually the leader of their community. He said, with that gravelly voice and generous smile, "Remember, you got me."

My experience has been that monks are very good at friendship. Friendship is considered something sacred and is not taken lightly by Benedictines. There was a time when young men and women in religious communities were taught to be wary of particular friendships. Fortunately, that season of religious formation has passed, and monastics are encouraged to build loving, stable friendships. But there was a core truth to the concern about particular friendships.

You don't have to be joined at the hip to be friends. People who work and live together, who are a part of each other's daily lives, gradually come into a sense of friendship even though they might not spend exclusive time with one another or do things together. Side by side we come to appreciate the beauty and rich terrain inside one another.

It is a slow dawning of friendship, and it takes on a different texture than close, personal friendships. However, the kind of friendship that Br. Ben gives, which is symbolized by monks' being pillows for one another, is one of the things most lacking in our culture. We remain strangers to those we are sharing time and space with.

All of us want to be accepted and known. This is most true in our most intimate relationships. But we need something more than strictly business from the others who inhabit our everyday world. We join clubs. We live in subdivisions. We sit in parishes.

We lack connection to others when there are people all around us.

This monastic way of understanding less intense but still crucial relationships could be called conviviality. Conviviality has to do with shared joy, work, and celebration. It is a festive way of doing life together and being together. It doesn't mean taking the weight of the world on your shoulders; it means throwing a party and extending hospitality within a warm tangle of relationships.

We'll get better at the particular friendships that are such great gifts to us when we get better at being present to all the familiar people who are also gifts of God.

Going Inward

Think about people you see every day. Those you work with, see on elevators or in stores. Is there a waiter or waitress who gets your coffee and sandwich every day? Is there a neighbor you wave to but haven't gotten to know? What about others? Postal clerk? Teacher? Club member?

For the next month, make an extra effort to speak with someone. Challenge yourself to accumulate as much knowledge about this person as you can. Concentrate on being more present, more aware of him or her in the ordinary encounters rather than trying to take the relationship outside its normal situation. You don't have to take your newspaper carrier out to lunch to become more aware of him.

For the next year, select someone every month to be more present to.

Holy Friend, there's not enough time in the world to be everyone's best friend. I need the ability to see the little, simple ways I can reach out to the familiar people I am doing life with. Help me notice when someone needs a kind or caring word. Stop me when I'm tempted to ignore others or take them for granted. Make me a friend. Amen.

17

LEADERSHIP

The Rule of St. Benedict

Whoever is abbot is to lead . . . by a twofold method: he must point out to those he leads all that is good and holy more by his own example than by words. . . . He is not to love one more than another . . . *for God shows no partiality among persons* (Rom. 2:11).

—*RB 2:11–12, 17, 20*

The abbot should not disturb the flock that is entrusted to his care or make any unfair arrangements, as though he had the power to do anything he wants.

—*RB 63:2*

The abbot must always remember the nature of his responsibility and remember the one to whom he will *give an account of his stewardship* (Luke 16:2). Let him remember that the well-being of those he serves (the monks) is his most important goal—not making a name for himself. . . . He should always pick mercy over judgment so that he too will receive mercy. . . . He should prune away their faults with wisdom and love as is best for each person. Let him strive to be loved rather than feared. . . . He must so arrange all things so that the strong have something to yearn after and the weak nothing to run from.

—*RB 64:7–15, 19*

Other Voices

The superiors, however, because they have to give an account to God for the souls entrusted to them, ought to exercise their authority in a spirit of service like Christ, whose place they hold in the monastery, safeguarding the respect owed to the human person.

The monastery prior is, above all, a shepherd of souls; that is, his office is above all spiritual. His authority assumes the character of humble service after the teaching and example of Christ. . . . Let the prior keep the person of every monk in great esteem, understand it and treat it with respect. Let his heart be open . . . the prior remains a brother among brothers in such way that, as a center of unity and charity, he gives himself to them totally."

—The American Priory
The Constitutions 1984:
Sylvestrine Congregation, o.s.b.

Dan

Before becoming a monk, Brother Damien ran his family's restaurant in Pontiac, Michigan. His story shows the leadership qualities and Benedictine values that were part of who Br. Damien was even when he was not a monk.

It wasn't unusual for Damien to provide meals for street people and hungry youth. However, he also wanted to teach them the value of work and would have them mop the floor, wash counters, or do some other basic task. The idea of work for food empowered the people Damien helped, and it built their dignity. He also hired people no one else would hire.

Sometimes these people did well at the chores they were given; sometimes they didn't. If someone failed to come up with a clean floor after mopping it, Damien would ask him or her to do it again. "You don't understand," he would say. "The children of God come in here. Is that floor clean enough for the children of God?" His leadership imparted dignity to the work, the worker, and the one served. It made holy the smallest task.

That is leadership at its best. Like the tenant farmers Jesus speaks of in the Gospels, we are stewards, not tyrants. We are servants, not lords. In practice, our roles of leadership might call on us to act and make choices on behalf of others. Even when our leadership roles are corporate or military in model, we can fulfill our obligations with the heart of a servant.

The responsibility we are given means that we put others before ourselves. Listen to people. Care about their lives. Pray for them. Dispense mercy. We are servants when we look out for the people who trust us, who lean on us. Sometimes a leader must do the hard thing for a higher good. Even this is servanthood if it is done with humility and genuine care for the welfare of others.

All of us have roles of leadership. At various times we are the boss, the parent, the captain, the president, the supervisor—or the prior, as in my present situation.

At our monastery I clean barns, mow lawns, and bale hay beside my brother monks. It's nothing extraordinary; that's just how monasteries work. Everyone gets a turn at kitchen duty, and everyone has to answer to someone. Benedict did not want the monastery superiors to be bullies or little monarchs. Families don't need bullies, and neither do schools, offices, stores, factories, churches, or any other organization. Neither the corporate model of leadership nor the military model of leadership is to be the model for Christians.

Servant leadership is the model of Jesus. Therefore, it is Benedict's model. Jesus acknowledged that in the systems we humans have built, those with power lord their leadership over others. "But not so with you," he said to his followers, "rather the greatest among you must become like . . . one who serves" (Luke 22:26).

To lead this way is to use our personal power—our advantage, you might say—to empower and serve others. We have the option of using this power selfishly and building an empire for ourselves. But we decide against it because we regard every other person we know as a daughter or son of God. Servant leadership goes against the status quo of our culture. The kingdom of God is a kingdom turned upside down, in which the king washes feet and the poor in spirit are the richest among us.

Going Inward

In what settings have you seen the two models of leadership (monarchy versus servant leadership) mentioned in this chapter? How do people respond to each model?

What are your own leadership roles? How do the people you lead respond to your style of leadership? Which model best describes your personal style? Is your style a conscious choice? Have you ever considered your influence over those you lead?

For the next month, pray for those who lead you. Pray for those you lead. If you know people who model servant leadership well, talk to them about it. Be sure to express your appreciation for what they do.

Jesus, there are various ways in which I lead others, just as there are various ways in which I follow the leadership of others. Leadership like yours seems a lofty ideal. But there you were in your dusty sandals surrounded by men who misunderstood you more often than they understood—yet you led them with tenderness and strength and love. You put them before yourself. I want to learn to do that. Amen.

18

COMMUNITY

The Rule of St. Benedict

There are four kinds of monks. First, there are the ceno-bites, . . . those who belong to a monastery, where they serve under a rule and leader. Second, there are the anchorites or hermits. . . . Third there are the sarabaites, . . . who have a character as soft as lead. . . . Two or three together, or even alone, without a shepherd, they pen themselves up in their own sheepfolds. . . . Their law is what they like to do, whatever strikes their fancy. . . . Fourth . . . there are gyrovagues, who spend their entire lives drifting from region to region. . . . Always on the move, they never settle down. . . . Let us pass by such living and with God's help draw up a plan for the strongest kind of monk, the cenobite.

—RB 1:1–13

On arising for the Work of God, prayer, the monks will quietly encourage each other, for the sleepy like to make excuses.

—RB 22:8

The workshop where we toil faithfully . . . is the shelter of the monastery and stability in the community.

—RB 4:78

Other Voices

There are a great many loose individuals in American society. . . . What makes this phenomenon of the "loose individual" most disturbing, however, is not simply the lack of relationships based on trust and responsibility, for there is obviously nothing particularly new about dishonesty, betrayal and infidelity. What is new is the fact that an increasing number of individuals actually *defend* infidelity and betrayal as the prerogatives of authentic selfhood. Indeed, the modern . . . ideal of absolute individual autonomy demands the freedom from even the possibility of moral judgment pronounced on the self.

—Craig M. Gay
The Way of the (Modern) World: Why It's Tempting to Live As If God Doesn't Exist

Monks get together in monasteries to follow Christ radically . . . There, in their monasteries, they enthusiastically seek the way to God, sharing

with each other the fruits of grace and fraternal
help. . . . Each Benedictine family is a living part
of the local church in which it strives to be a sign
of the divine presence.

For we ought to recognize legitimate pluralism,
that is, diversity among members gathered
together. . . . It is not permissible to suppress the
variety of skills or of intellectual powers under the
cloak of unity. In the monastery . . . each has his
own gift, but the light of the Spirit may be given
to anyone for the good of all. The diversity of the
members becomes useful to the whole body.
Individuals can share the fullness of the Spirit
only by sharing in the communion of the different gifts.

—The American Priory
The Constitutions 1984:
Sylvestrine Congregation, o.s.b.

Lonni

Benedict's description of four kinds of monks could
also be thought of as four kinds of people. It's
important to realize that such sweeping statements
are effective only because they are generalizations.
Obviously, the diversity among us as human beings is

more complicated than such a statement would indicate, and so is the diversity among monks.

What's interesting, though, is that Benedict bases his observations on community. The monks are defined by their relationships. Cenobites are commended; they are the monks who live in community. The hermits, who live alone, have grown to this advanced stage of spirituality by first living at length in community. Benedict describes them as having "come through the test of living a long time in a monastery . . . they have built up their strength and go from the battle line in the ranks of their brothers."

Benedict casts the blame for the sorry state of the sarabaites' and gyrovagues' character and spirituality on their failure to stay put, belong to a community, and yield to any force or law outside the personal self.

Individualism is an icon in Western culture. We attribute it to cowboys and heroes and martyrs. Benedict shows us a better way.

One summer morning several years ago, I arrived at the monastery early for Sunday morning Mass. As I pulled into the long, tree-lined drive, my way was blocked by a couple of vans and a car. There were large cameras being unloaded, the kind you'd make a commercial with. It was eight in the morning, and it was Sunday. Seemed a little strange. The drivers politely pulled to the side and let me pass.

Almost immediately, I ran into Brother Gregory, the monastery administrator, and asked about the vans and cameras. Concern clouded his face.

"Cameras?"

"Big ones," I replied.

"Vans?"

"Two."

"In the driveway? I haven't heard anything about anything like that." (It turned out that a car company was photographing, with permission, and word of the event had not yet reached Br. Gregory.)

He rose up to his full height and immediately went into guard-dog mode. It is part of his job to guard and oversee the resources of the community. When I looked into the eyes of this quiet, gentle man I saw something fiercely protective. It was born out of his sense of community. He would protect the monastery the way a father protects his children or a big sister her little brother. Community inspired the hero in Br. Gregory.

Something happens to us in our living together that can't happen if we choose isolation. What we give and get in community makes us substantially stronger people. "I come away stronger," said one friend when talking about her community of faith.

"I believe in the love that you gave me / I believe in the faith that can save me / I believe in the hope / and I pray that someday it may raise me / Above these badlands," wrote and sang Bruce Springsteen. "Badlands" will happen.

The love that has been given to us, the faith that is the legacy of those who have gone before us—these things can get us through. But the "loose individual" will find little to hold to and no one to give her the strength she needs to "keep pushin' . . . till these badlands start treating us good."

Going Inward

How are you involved in a faith community? Determine what actions you need to take to strengthen those ties.

In what circumstance did your involvement in community make you "come away stronger"?

Who are the people who have most influenced your spiritual formation? Find a way to tell them about their impact on your life.

Look again at Benedict's four kinds of monks. Which of these would best describe you? Why?

Are there any "badlands" in your life that might be helped by deeper involvement with community?

God, relationships with others seem like a mixed bag to me. However, I desire the fortitude, power, and companionship of community. Help me see how others can help me get through the hard times; remind me of how others have shaped me into the person I am and the person I am becoming. Let me become more conscious of the power of my relationships. Teach me to engage myself fully with the people in my life. Amen.

19

PERSEVERANCE

The Rule of St. Benedict

Those who are patient while enduring difficulty and injustice are fulfilling the Lord's command.

—RB 7:42

This is the good zeal that monks must cultivate with earnest love . . . enduring with the greatest patience one another's weaknesses of body or behavior.

—RB 72:3–5

And finally, never lose hope.

—RB 4:74

Other Voices

I believe in the sun even when it is not shining.

I believe in love even when feeling it not.

I believe in God even when He is silent.

—An inscription on a wall in a cellar in Cologne, Germany, where Jews hid from the Nazis

Lonni

E nter through the heavy wooden door into the monastery with me. I want to show you the faces of perseverance.

There's Brother Ben. He's eighty-five this month. He can't hear anymore, and he can't eat the same food the rest of the monks eat because of his health, and there's talk that maybe no one will want to keep the cows after he's gone. Bad news to a cowboy. But he's still there for the breaking of bread every morning, and he still works in the barn, still delivers calves. Every day he's the first to Mass. Those aren't lines you see on his face. Those are the traces of perseverance.

Brother Antony. When he arrived at the monastery many years ago, he found a place filled with men old enough to be his father or grandfather. He was the sole hope, the seed of a beginning. He stayed when others would have lost hope. Eventually, younger men came. And when they did, among the faces of the old men they found the young, strong, determined face of Br. Antony.

There is Brother Greg, who will fix dinner for the three hundredth time this year. Father Mike, who will tell the same joke for the three hundredth time—and still believe someone might laugh. Talk about perseverance.

All together, all of them, the young men and the old men will go into the chapel one more time because they believe it means something. Let the idiots say that the monastic way of life is archaic and insignificant— the monks will keep showing up. When one more novice comes and goes, when they bury one of their brothers, when the nights are long and lonely, when friends are few—the monks on the hill will persevere.

If this sounds like drudgery, you aren't getting it. The faces aren't hard faces or sour ones or bitter ones. Look into those eyes around the monastery table, and you'll see joy. Yes, there are losses and there is difficulty. "But God never said we'd be leading at the half," Father Dan says, quoting an old book title.

Monastic perseverance is rich with hope. There are chapels to build, dreams to dream, souls to heal, parties to host, stories to tell, people to love, places to go, and things to do. In the midst of an abiding perseverance, there will be monastic revelry as well.

Several years ago, I attended the simple profession of one of the monks. During dinner I sat to the left of Fr. Dan. On his right was Father Noel (who has since died).

Fr. Noel was very old and very Italian. In order to facilitate conversation, Fr. Dan would, under his breath and with sensitive subtlety, translate Fr. Noel's broken English words for me. Fr. Noel and I would both lean across Fr. Dan, planted solidly between us, to converse. I'm sure Fr. Dan thought he was needed in this capacity, and frankly, he seemed to enjoy his role even though I understood Fr. Noel just fine (but I didn't tell Fr. Dan that until years later).

After dinner, the guests were mingling as the party was winding down. Fr. Noel walked up to me and took both my hands in his. He smiled a dazzling smile, motioned with his head toward Fr. Dan, who was across the room talking to a couple, and said, "So, dear lady, now we can really talk, yes?"

Most often, perseverance simply means outlasting whatever is getting in the way.

Going Inward

Determine a circumstance in your life that calls for perseverance. What is getting in the way? What steps do you need to take to strengthen your perseverance and get the obstacle out of your way?

Think about a time when you gritted your teeth and persevered in a difficult situation. Write about it in your journal or tell someone about it.

Why did you do it? What did you learn about yourself and others? What situations now exist that call for the same kind of perseverance?

How are humor, realistic expectations, and faith involved in the ability to persevere?

Send a note of encouragement to someone who is persevering, perhaps using the quote from the cellar in Germany.

God, I don't want to give up. Perseverance *isn't a word I hear much. But I want to persevere. Give me the perseverance of St. Benedict and hold me up in spite of all that would cause me to collapse and give up. I put my trust in you to keep me persevering for the long haul. Amen.*

20

BALANCE AND CELEBRATION

The Rule of St. Benedict

Arrange all things so that the strong have something to yearn after and the weak nothing to run from.

—*RB 64:19*

Other Voices

Jesus shares with us the darkness of what it is to be without God as well as showing forth the glory of what it is to be with God. He speaks about it, and perhaps that is much of why, although we have not followed him very well these past two thousand years or so, we have never quite been able to stop listening to him. We listen almost in spite of ourselves when he tells us the ship is sinking with all hands aboard. All of you labor and are heavy laden, he says. It is an appalling thing to tell us when we are trying so hard to pretend that it is not so.

—Frederick Buechner
Telling the Truth: The Gospel as Tragedy, Comedy, and Fairy Tale

Dan

My father was a milkman. Before I thought of becoming a monk, I thought of being a milkman or maybe a mailman (it seemed similar). My father died years ago, and nothing has ever filled the place he left. I learned many important things from Dad. Some of them are easy to articulate, and some I've just had to try and live. Balance is difficult to articulate; you just have to live it.

Whatever my father did, he did completely. On his softball team, he played with a ferocious intensity. He understood what work was for. He enjoyed his work and the people he served. Dad learned the customers' names, patted the children, even got on ground level to play with them. He loved his family. When he was with Mom and us six kids, he was altogether with us. He'd hold my mother on his lap, and we'd all pile on top.

I remember seeing him kneeling by his bed. I can't even begin to imagine how it influenced me—knowing that the strongest man in the world prayed. There is a time for every thing under the sun. Dad knew it. He taught it to me in his actions and in the way he lived.

Benedict understood balance too. He is careful to articulate that there must be time for everything. Work. Sleep. Food. Companionship. Solitude. Noise. Silence. Reading.

We get out of balance when we spend too much of ourselves in just one activity. The person who can't shut the door to work will soon burn out. Too much solitude makes us self-absorbed. Too much play makes us fools. Too much sleep and food, and we become lazy. Too much activity, and our souls become threadbare.

A while back, a newspaper reported the story of a beautiful, intelligent, wealthy woman who was known to be ambitious and singularly focused on her career. She was a powerful woman in her field. She was respected. She had it all: houses, cars, and a big bank account. One day she left her office and drove to a hotel, where she killed herself. She left a note saying that she was "tired of clapping with one hand."

When we've lost a sense of balance, it feels like trying to clap with one hand. It takes a full life, a balanced life, to sound the noise of celebration. Hands that work, love, play, pray, give, rest—hands like that can also clap joyfully.

Going Inward

Are you ever the person who can't shut the door to work? Do you withdraw too often? Do you ever worry about spending too much energy, time, and resources on something? In what ways and in what situations do you tend to extremes?

Think of one situation in which you would like to strike a better balance. What specific steps can you take toward that goal?

Lord, I bring you my extremes and my lacks. There are deeper motivations for my obsessions and my complacency than I know or understand. But you plunge into the depths of my heart, and you know things about me that I can hardly name. Take my life and give me balance. Amen.

21

JOY

The Rule of St. Benedict

As we journey in this way of life and in faith, we shall run on the path . . . our hearts overflowing with the inexpressible delight of love.

—RB Prologue: 49

They should sleep clothed, . . . but they should remove their knives, lest they accidentally cut themselves.

—RB 22:5

Do not pamper yourself.

—RB 4:12

Other Voices

You say you see no hope, you say you see no reason
We should dream that the world would ever change
You're saying love is foolish to believe
Cause there'll always be some crazy with an Army or a Knife

*To wake you from your day dream, put the fear back
in your life . . .*

Look, if someone wrote a play just to glorify
*What's stronger than hate, would they not arrange
the stage*
*To look as if the hero came too late, he's almost in
defeat*
It's looking like the Evil side will win, so on the edge
*Of every seat, from the moment that the whole thing
begins*
It is . . .

(Chorus)
Love who makes the mortar
And it's love who stacked these stones
And it's love who made the stage here
Although it looks like we're alone
In this scene set in shadows
Like the night is here to stay
There is evil cast around us

But it's love that wrote the play . . .
For in this darkness love can show the way.

So now the stage is set. Feel your own heart beating
In your chest. This life's not over yet.
So we get up on our feet and do our best. We play
against the Fear.
We play against the reasons not to try.
We're playing for the tears burning in the happy
angel's eyes.
For it's . . . (Chorus)

—David Wilcox
"Show the Way"

Lonni and Dan

If we believe that love did indeed "stack the stones," wouldn't there be less fear and more joy? There's no denying that there is a lot to fear, and it's hard to be joyful when you're choking on fear.

But joy isn't something that simply happens to us. Joy is a decision we have to make—or not. You and I are responsible for whether or not we experience joy. Joy isn't going to happen if we pamper ourselves. Instead, we need to consider what is preventing the joy.

There are a lot of things that can choke joy, but here are ten to think about:

1. Fear

2. Cynicism

3. Boredom

4. Low self-esteem

5. Taking life too seriously

6. Loss of wonder

7. Greed

8. Guilt

9. Bitterness

10. Busyness

Harboring any of these is a lot like taking your knife to bed. It's like saying, "Don't put that broken glass in your bed; you'll cut yourself." You can't sleep with fear. It'll do more than keep you awake at night; it'll wound you.

Knives aren't just weapons, though; knives are also about self-defense. The things we do that choke joy are often about self-defense. The universe doesn't seem safe.

We aren't sure it's friendly out there. As Wilcox says, "There'll always be some crazy with an Army or a Knife."

But if love is the ultimate reality, if love "wrote the play" and "set the stage," maybe we can give ourselves to love rather than to fear. Jesus told us that love drives away fear. When we take to the highways of life with the determination to love, joy will find us.

Going Inward

Review the list of joy chokers, thinking about which ones are yours. Consider why you picked the ones you did. What can you do about the joy chokers?

Is there some fear you have never discussed with anyone? What is your greatest fear, and what is the basis of that fear? How could love relieve the fear and make space for joy?

Faithful Father, you have seen into the depths of me. There's no reason to hide anything from you or to pretend that I am what I'm not or that I have no fears. The antidote to fear is not courage; it is love. Make me more loving. Open me to your love. Take this callused heart of mine and break it if you must. I won't fear love. Teach me to love. Amen.

22

SIMPLE
AUTHENTICITY

The Rule of St. Benedict

Your way of acting should be different from the world's way.

—*RB 4:20*

For daily meals, whatever time, it is enough . . . to provide all tables with two kinds of cooked food because of the individual preferences. In this way, the person who may not be able to eat one kind of food may partake of the other. Two kinds of cooked foods therefore should suffice . . . , and if fruit or fresh vegetables are available, a third dish may be added.

—*RB 39:1–3*

Other Voices

Seldom or never do we hear anything about simplicity as an essential discipline of the spiritual life. Most of us have only a vague idea of the meaning of the word. Perhaps, we had better begin with a definition. Simplicity means "absence of artificial ornamentation or pretentious styles . . . lack of cunning or duplicity." Where there is simplicity words can be taken at their face value. There are no hidden or double meanings. . . . Where there is simplicity there is no artificiality. One does not try to appear younger, or wiser, or richer than one is. . . . Love makes no parade and gives itself no airs.

—Albert Day
Discipline and Discovery

Though we're strangers still I love you
I love you more than your mask
And you know that you must trust this to be true
And I know that's much to ask

—Rich Mullins

Lonni

S implicity is trendy. People have shelves of books and attend conferences lasting a day or longer to learn how to downsize the clutter and complexity of their lives. This is one time when the cliché "Just do it" seems appropriate.

My husband and I often have visitors to our cabin during the summer. Late one night around the bonfire, the conversation turned to luxury. We talked about how all of us have more than we need. One man said he had at least twenty-five sweaters. Another talked about his expensive hobby. A woman mentioned the clothes in her closet. She said a lot of them have never had the price tags taken off, and "the stuff is at least a year old." About this time someone spoke up and said, "But it's our American right to overspend and consume. That's why we go to college—to make the big bucks and accumulate."

It isn't just our dressers and closets and pole barns that are jammed. That's the easy part to simplify. You just square your shoulders and cut back. The harder part? Ceasing all of our complicated artificiality.

It is as if it comes naturally to us to disguise ourselves. We are master shape-changers, and we learn it young. We learn it from the first hurts, the times when somehow it was not enough to be ourselves. With all the beauty and magic that is in us, we learn to lift a mask to our faces, we hide the tears, we tone down the laughter, and we start believing that all skies should be colored blue.

The bigger problem, and maybe the root of why we accumulate, has to do with the clutter in our minds and hearts. Our relationships are cluttered, and our energy is fragmented in all directions.

Billy Joel sings that he doesn't know why he goes to extremes. We relate to what he's saying. We all wonder what's wrong inside of us that we can't get a grip on ourselves.

Keeping to the basics—this is the strength of the Benedictine life. And it starts with the courage to step out of the disguise and into the reality of who we are. It starts with dropping the masks, simplifying our words, our actions, our relationships. When we are authentically ourselves, we won't need the ornamentation, exaggeration, or accumulation.

Benedict says that you should offer two kinds of cooked food for the main meal. This down-to-earth section of the Rule speaks sanely, directly, and clearly. Attention to the details, appreciation of the small things, sensitivity to personal preferences—these are all favored by Benedict. At the same time, his rule for life insists that we not go to extremes.

Even though it's a lot to ask, we are to believe that there is love in the universe packed into and overflowing in the snowflakes and the sunrises and the birdcalls and the touch of a friend. We are to believe it enough to take off the mask. No, it's not easy. We aren't going to get it right the first time we try. But keep trying and don't stop believing. There's a title of a Benedictine book that says it well: "Always we begin again."

Going Inward

I have this instinct, this bell that goes off inside when I am being anything other than who I really am. You have it too. I hear it too often, and I've gotten pretty good at turning the bell off or rationalizing the words or behavior that are not authentic.

For the next few days, try to be attentive to the interior sound that signals when you are being less than authentic. Pay attention to the moment and what caused you to assume the disguise.

There is no effortless way and no instant fix for the problem of masquerading. The first and most important step is training ourselves to pay attention to what we're doing and saying and to why we are doing and saying these things.

Don't let the moment pass without examining it. As you become more aware of the ways you play dress-up, you will begin the tough process of living simply.

Loving God, I give you my masks, my disguises. That's not to say I won't snatch one back now and then. But at this moment, and with a heart full of the right intention, I hand over this box of pretense and receive from you the full dignity of authenticity. I know there's a lot for me to learn about being real. I want to start now. Amen.

23

LECTIO DIVINA (SACRED READING)

The Rule of St. Benedict

The Lord says in the Gospel: *Whoever hears these words of mine and does them is like a wise man who built his house upon rock; the floods came and the winds blew and beat against the house, but it did not fall: it was founded on rock* (Matt. 7:24–25). . . . The Lord waits for us daily to translate into action, as we should, his holy teachings.

—*RB Prologue:33–35*

Divine Scripture calls to us.

—*RB 7:1*

They will devote themselves to their reading or to the psalms.

—*RB 48:13*

Other Voices

We all have the capability and the grace to become masters in the art of sacred reading, although there are special challenges to be faced in our post-literate age. . . . The high value monks have placed on sacred reading comes from the conviction that in this practice we meet God through the instrumentality of the divine word. Before the fifteenth century there were no periods set aside in the monastic schedule for meditative prayer. The common way of communing with God was sacred reading; this was the monastic method of meditation. The monk or nun would sit with the text of Scripture and begin to read attentively and reflectively until a word or phrase or scene struck the imagination or the heart.

At that moment the reader paused, put the text aside, and gave himself to prayer . . . When I spend time in sacred reading I invite God's word to penetrate my heart and to evoke from that deepest center of my being a response of surrender, wonder, praise, regret, petition, love. In the words I read God speaks to me; in my prayerful pauses I respond to God, verbally or wordlessly . . . the process is a gentle one. The Lord does not come in an earthquake but in a soft, whispering sound (1 Kings 19:22). . . . The encounter is real without being extraordinary or spectacular.

. . . Repeated encounters with the word of God will bring about a gradual transformation as my thinking and willing become progressively harmonized with God's will. Slowly I grow in interior freedom and lose my innate orientation towards comfort and security.

> —Charles Cummings, o.c.s.o.
> *Monastic Practices*

Lonni

The theory behind Lectio, commonly called sacred reading, is a unique one. It begins with the assumption that human beings are equipped with the ability to hear God. Not just monks and nuns, saints and mystics. You and me. Your kid, your neighbor, your boss, the person who bags your groceries.

The origins of Lectio are clearly monastic. Father Dan is hesitant to say that it is, in origin, a Benedictine tradition. However, that's what our research indicates. To learn more, we suggest you pick from the reading list one of the books that has a good section on the topic of Lectio.

The world is a cacophony of sound. How do we sort through the voices and figure out which one is God's? Lectio is one way. Lectio places us in a direct encounter with God's Word. We learn the sound of it—the subtleties, the rhythms, the language of God.

Before telling you the how of Lectio, let me explain why I think this chapter is the most important one you'll read. Lectio is so basic to Benedictine spirituality that if you miss this, you've missed the heart of it.

Lectio teaches us to listen. Benedictine spirituality is about listening to God and listening to life. Lectio eventually moves us beyond reading Scripture to reading our lives, to reading our world. The important, core idea here is listen. Listen.

A little while after beginning Lectio, you discover that movies speak God, music speaks God, your friends become prophetic oracles. God begins to speak so persistently in all of life that you awake every day amazed that you didn't hear all this God-noise before. Lectio opens the ears of your heart.

After some practice, all of life will speak to you of God. But there is no substitute for God's holy word in the Bible. Specific times must be set aside for the experience of opening Scripture, and this must remain the core of the Lectio experience. It cannot be abandoned when you begin to hear God more and more.

There are four phases to the rhythm of Lectio: reading, meditation, prayer, and contemplation. Don't think about this legalistically and worry that you aren't giving enough attention to each phase. While the process can be organized into four steps, it is better viewed as a whole, as a rhythm with harmonies that flow into one another and drift together.

Reading is the leisurely, prayerful attention to the text in which you grasp the meaning of the text. It is done very slowly. Reading out loud helps decelerate the usual habit of reading quickly to glean information. Read until some word or phrase takes hold of you.

Then go with it. Spend time with it, roll it over, wrap yourself completely around it, and let it penetrate you to the core. Let it get to you. That's the second stage. In the third stage (prayer), attention shifts from the text to God. The text leads you to an awareness of God's being with you, God's speaking to you in the text, and this evokes a response to God.

The fourth stage is a quiet resting in God's presence. There's a wonderful story about a farmer who prays with monks every morning, and after prayer he just sits in the pew and stares. One day a monk asks him what he's doing. He replies, "I look at God, and he looks at me."

That's it. When you've completed the cycle, if you have time, go back to the text and continue reading. For however long you set aside for Lectio you can expect to enter a cycle of reading, meditating, praying, and contemplating. It becomes easier to listen to the text as you stay with it and practice. It is a simple exercise, but it is not easy. It will take time.

Gradually, something happens inside people who practice Lectio. Relationships become truer, sharp edges are softened, and we become kinder, gentler, more considerate, and less likely to bite, gossip, and act on our most selfish impulses. We are converted by the Word, which speaks to us.

The lived reality of Lectio is really very simple. Don't let the books or methodology intimidate you. It is about listening and responding. It is about expecting to hear God. You were created with the ability to hear God. It comes in the human equipment.

Lectio is prayer. Anyone can pray. When you open the Bible, that's prayer. When you open yourself to the text, that's prayer too. Lectio is all about a relationship with a God who is not silent. God is speaking and wants us to hear. Lectio teaches us to listen.

Going Inward

Commit yourself to practicing Lectio for six months. Tell someone about your plans and ask that person to inquire about your progress occasionally. Begin with one of these New Testament books: James, Philippians, or the Gospel of Luke.

Keep a Lectio notebook in which you write down, in a few simple sentences, what you experienced during Lectio.

Try using Lectio when reading the passages from the Rule of St. Benedict that are quoted at the beginning of each chapter. St. Benedict suggests to his monks that they practice Lectio on the writings of the Fathers, the Catholic classics of the day. In our age, Benedict is certainly a spiritual father.

Father, open the ears of my heart. Give me faith to believe that I am fully equipped to hear you. Quiet me enough to notice your stirring in my depths. Teach me to listen. Amen.

24

WISDOM

The Rule of St. Benedict

As often as anything important is to be done in the monastery, the abbot shall call the whole community together and himself explain what the business is; and after hearing the advice of the brothers, let him ponder it and follow what he judges the wiser course.

—RB 3:1–2

We urge that if anyone finds this arrangement of psalms unsatisfactory, they should arrange whatever they judge to be better.

—RB 18:22

There ought to be an appropriate proportion between the seriousness of a fault and the measure of discipline.

—RB 24:1

The abbot must exercise the utmost care and concern for the wayward because *it is not the healthy who need a physician . . .* (Matt. 9:12). He ought to use every skill of a wise physician and send in . . . mature and wise brothers who, under the cloak of secrecy, may support the wavering brother, urge him to be humble . . . , and *console* him *lest he be overwhelmed by excessive sorrow* (2 Cor. 2:7).

—*RB 27:1–3*

Other Voices

To grasp God in all things—this is the sign of your new birth.

—Meister Eckhart

Ring the bells that still can ring
Forget your perfect offering
There is a crack in everything
That's how the light gets in

—Leonard Cohen
Stranger Music

Lonni

I loved books as a child, and my favorite stories were about lost kingdoms, lost thrones, lost loves, and how courage, perseverance, and faith worked together, against all odds, to discover the thing that was lost. Usually something wicked rearranges the world of the child in the story so that the child doesn't know the truth about who she is. She thinks herself a pauper or a slave when she was actually born to nobility, honor, and beauty.

As the child grows, she happens into some moment of grace in which she realizes who she is. It is a gift given to her by a Benevolence that has never left her and never forgotten her. The deep wisdom she acquires gives her the courage to redeem what has been lost. It is never easy for her after that graced moment, but she is never the same either. The kind of genuine knowing that is classically called wisdom gives her something substantial to hold on to even when evil roars in her face.

Today, Americans are looking for lost wisdom. Ancient books of "wisdom" are increasingly popular. People are looking for old answers to new dilemmas. The search reminds me of those enchanted stories. We don't know who we are anymore. Some evil has caused us to forget that we are born of the substance of the stars and glory of God. We're looking for the lost wisdom, but we're looking in many of the wrong places.

Wisdom recognizes the two basic truths expressed in the "Other Voices" section: God is present in all things, and the cracks that run through everything—those little imperfections—are the places where light will shine. We don't need perfection; we just need to make room for the light to creep through the cracks. Our lost kingdoms are always redeemable. Wisdom will tell you that. It will sing hope and redemption in the darkest night. It will expand our souls enough for the light to erupt.

The passage in Benedict's Rule about the abbot sending the wise and mature brothers to the one who has been corrected is a wonderful example of light getting through the cracks. It has a magical, enchanted sense to it. It also reveals a great deal about the heart and wisdom of Benedict. On one hand, it's a monastery after all, and "anything goes" will not do.

However, rules or not, Benedict is not going to sit by and let anyone be broken by discouragement. Yes, he wants those who have the authority to correct others to use that power when appropriate, but he wants the one who has been corrected to feel supported, consoled, and encouraged. He doesn't want to crush anyone. This is just one example of the astute and durable wisdom that infuses every word of the Rule. There's nothing ethereal about Benedict's brand of wisdom. It is down-to-earth.

It's important that we understand that information does not make anyone wise. To be clever is not to be wise; to be informed or educated is not to be wise. Contrivances are not wisdom, and neither is technology or philosophy. Wisdom doesn't show off what it knows. It gives itself away in those enchanted, graceful moments when we need it most. It is life giving. Wisdom is also recognized by its practicality. It is usable. It feels more like a solid oak rocker than it does a lounge chair. How can it be enchanted *and* practical? Only wisdom could pull it off. Imitations fade against the standard.

Going Inward

Talk to at least two people about what *wisdom* means. Compare their answers with your own thoughts on the subject.

Who is the wisest person you know? What makes him or her wise? How do you recognize that wisdom?

In what specific situation do you now need wisdom? How will you get it?

Think about three ways you can grow in wisdom. This list will help you think about the ways you might grow or have already grown in wisdom.

- Books about spirituality
- Prayer

- Serious discussion with others
- Experience
- Education
- Observation and attention
- Application of truth
- Faith
- Spiritual disciplines
- Lectio Divina
- Service
- Relationships

Holy Wisdom, come to me. Leak through the cracks and bind up the wounds. Turn on the light in my darkness. Amen.

25

SPIRITUAL
DISCIPLINE

The Rule of St. Benedict

We must run and do now what will profit us forever.

—*RB Prologue:44*

Their law is what they like to do, whatever strikes their fancy. Anything they believe in and choose, they call holy; anything they dislike, they consider forbidden.

—*RB 1:8–9*

Other Voices

God does not demand that we give up our personal dignity . . . that we lose ourselves and turn from all that is not him. God needs nothing, asks nothing, and demands nothing, like the stars. It is life with God which demands these things. . . . God does not, I regret to report, give a hoot. You do not have to do these things—unless you want to know God. They work on you, not on him.

You do not have to sit outside in the dark. If, however, you want to look at the stars, you will find that darkness is necessary. But the stars neither require nor demand it.

—Annie Dillard
Teaching a Stone to Talk

> The monk who forgets God, forgets himself.
>
> —Michael Casey

> Saying no to yourself is the beginning of freedom.
>
> —Richard Rohr

Dan

When I was growing up, my dad was a door-to-door milkman. My brothers and I could hardly wait to be old enough (eight, he said) to go along and help him. What a thrill to carry even one quart of milk for him. We enjoyed just being with our father, and as we got older and stronger, we were actually of help to him.

But what was really thrilling and memorable was the look in the eyes of coworkers, customers, even customers' children, when they discovered I was Frank Homan's son. The look conveyed instant respect. Now, my brothers and I knew we had not done anything to earn their respect, but it made us want to become people who merited that kind of respect.

That's how it is in our relationship with God. We have inherent dignity, but becoming people of integrity and authentic spirituality takes work and attention to our lives. The spiritual disciplines are tools by which we cooperate with God in the building of our personhood. As St. Paul, St. Benedict, and many others have said, we need to live lives worthy of our inheritance and call as the children of God.

With an identity like that, we are responsible to care for ourselves, each other, and our world. What we do with our minds, hearts, bodies, and souls—this matters. To exclaim "Yes!" to life and the prospects of life is a gift we have because of who we are. But to say that all-important yes, we will have to say no to whatever chokes, or threatens to choke, life out of us. Our yes to prayer is a no to some distraction. Our yes to service is a no to selfishness. Our yes to fidelity is a no to duplicity.

My dad delivered more than milk. Milk helps with physical nourishment, but Dad delivered care, genuine concern, and a good word for everybody. His work was a spiritual discipline for him. He was good for people's souls. And we knew how he got that way. He received nourishment from Mom's love and from his God, his Father and friend.

Discipline has little to do with willpower and everything to do with self-worth. Whether it is the discipline of prayer or fasting or kindness, we do it because we are the children of God and because our worth comes with a hardy responsibility.

The healthiest discipline and self-esteem are established in our identity as God's sons and daughters. Discipline based on this high naming of us as God's children is discipline with joy. The kind of joy a little boy discovers when he finds out it is a privilege to be his father's son.

Going Inward

Author Richard Foster categorizes the classic spiritual disciplines this way:

- Inward disciplines—meditation, prayer, fasting, study
- Outward disciplines—simplicity, solitude, submission, service
- Corporate disciplines—confession, worship, guidance, celebration

With which of these disciplines do you have experience? Which are you most interested in? Which would be most difficult for you? Pick one from each category to integrate as a means of spiritual growth for the next three months. Do not begin with all three at once, but add one each month.

Read *Celebration of Discipline* by Richard Foster. If it is not on the shelf of your local bookstore, place a special order.

How can saying no to yourself be the beginning of freedom?

God, you know me better than I know myself. I'm sure there are things I need to say no to and things I need to learn to say yes to. I don't know where to begin. If I look at the big picture, it is discouraging. I need your help. Please direct me. Amen.

26

OBEDIENCE

The Rule of St. Benedict

We must prepare our hearts and bodies for the battle of holy obedience to his instructions. What is possible to us naturally, let us ask the Lord to supply.

—*RB Prologue:40–41*

In the monastery no one is to follow their own heart's desire, nor shall anyone presume to contend . . . defiantly.

—*RB 3:8*

The first step of humility is unhesitating obedience.

—*RB 5:1*

This very obedience, however, . . . is not cringing or sluggish or half-hearted, but free from any grumbling or any reaction of unwillingness.

—*RB 5:14*

The brothers should serve one another.

—*RB 35:1*

Other Voices

> The essence of obedience is putting others before myself. This means that we obey everyone, not only those who are placed in authority over us. In this sense it is not a virtue peculiar to monasteries but is an indispensable ingredient in all relations. A mother obeys her child by getting up in the middle of the night to feed it or to quiet its crying. A father obeys his family by going out to work. . . . It is love in action.
>
> —Cyprian Smith, O.S.B.
> *The Path of Life: Benedictine Spirituality for Monks and Lay People*

Lonni and Dan

No one wants to obey anyone else anymore. To suggest it is considered insulting to our autonomy, our intelligence, and our maturity. We've shot and buried the word *obey,* replacing it with words that don't have the same tone of authoritarianism. But in real life, every person who has loving relationships and solid working relationships obeys.

The Latin root of the word *obedience* is *ob audire;* it means "to listen." We get *audio* from it also. If we stick with this meaning, *obey* becomes less harsh on the contemporary ear.

There's good reason the word *obey* causes a shudder to course through us: The concept has been used to keep people down, to coerce and control others. Women and children, specifically, have endured atrocities in the name of obedience. St. Benedict's use of the word reflects that he was a man of his culture. His view of authority was stern, though very progressive for his day because it involved love.

Whatever seems unacceptably authoritarian to our contemporary ears is balanced by this one sentence: "The brothers [and sisters] should serve one another."

Benedict differed from earlier monastic writers in this. Often such writers set up the abbot as just beneath God, and his word was to hold as much authority. Benedict too wanted the community leaders to be heard, respected, and obeyed. But he also wanted the prior or abbot or leaders to listen. Listen to the young, he said. They will often have important insights.

In other words, everyone should obey everyone else, listen to everyone else. If we do not—sooner or later— love and yield to other human beings, we will never learn to love and yield to God, whom we cannot see. As uneasy as we are with the word itself, obedience is the key to lasting and healthy relationships. But it only works when we love and serve mutually, without conditions.

Certainly a rule is reasonably expected to legislate behavior. But Benedict found it repulsive to merely conform and never have one's heart converted. He knew that rules would not solve all the problems and would not draw the monk closer to God. The standards for monastic observance are not lowered in Benedict's Rule, but the motivation behind obedience or any monastic value is Benedict's main concern. He was going for inner transformation rather than outward compliance.

At the beginning of the movie *Les Miserables,* a man is dying in a gutter. He had been imprisoned for stealing bread when he was hungry, and now he is an ex-prisoner. He is an outcast.

He goes to a church for help, where a compassionate priest gives him food and a warm bed and tries to encourage him. In the middle of the night, the ex-prisoner steals silverware, punches the priest, and escapes into the night. He is returned the next day by the local authorities, who triumphantly tell the priest that the man had the audacity to claim that the silverware had been a gift. They are obviously eager for the priest to denounce the thief.

The priest says he is glad they have brought him back and turns to the frightened man, who is certain he's about to be condemned. The priest asks him, "But, my friend, I also gave you the silver candlesticks. Why did you leave them behind?" None of us would deny that the priest had every right to have the guy hauled off to jail. It was a right he didn't use, a power he denied himself for the good of the other man.

That is the spirit of Benedict's obedience. Selflessness. It does not insist on its rights and is not always defending itself. It can give something away for the good of another. It aids the process of extraordinary conversion.

Obedience is the monk who awakes in the hours before dawn and goes once more to the print shop where he helps make a living for the rest of his community. It is the monk who bales hay year after year and the monk who cleans when he'd rather be reading, painting, or running. It is the brother who makes candles for thousands of retreat youth when he will hardly ever meet those kids or see their candlelit young faces made peaceful by the sacrament of reconciliation. These are all acts of obedience by real-life monks, men who could insist on their right to say no. You and I who aren't monks, we obey in similar ways every day.

The test of our obedience is simple. Love is the test. The depth and width and breadth of our ability to love are measured by how much we love the one who is tough to love. The same is true of obedience, submission, yielding, whatever you call it. If we have learned how to obey, we will do it when it is not easy, when it costs us something. As long as we clutch the silver candlesticks in our white-knuckled fist, we have not learned obedience—or love.

Going Inward

What is your initial reaction to the word *obedience?* Why? How does the monastic vision of obedience apply to you?

Thinking of obedience as "love in action," try to be aware of opportunities and situations in which you can obey. Look for examples around you also.

Look for an opportunity to help someone else rethink the value and meaning of obedience.

Jesus, they say that you obeyed to the point of death. You held nothing back but gave everything. I need to rethink my ideas about obedience. The word makes me uneasy. But I am learning to listen, so if obedience means listening to you and listening to others, I can do that. Listening was really important to St. Benedict. Give me a listening heart that won't resist obedience. Amen.

27

WORDS

The Rule of St. Benedict

Never offer a hollow greeting of peace or turn away when someone needs your love. Bind yourself to no oath lest it prove false, but speak the truth with heart and tongue. . . . Do not grumble or speak ill of others.

—RB 4:25–28, 39–40

Prefer moderation in speech and speak no foolish chatter.

—RB 4:52–53

There are times when good words are to be left unsaid out of esteem for silence.

—RB 6:2

A monk speaks gently . . . and with becoming modesty, briefly and reasonably, but without raising his voice.

—RB 7:60

Let us consider how we should behave in the presence of God . . . and let us stand . . . in such a way that our minds are in harmony with our voices.

—RB 19:6

First and most importantly, there must be no word or sign of the evil of grumbling, no manifestation of it for any reason.

—*RB 34:6*

Other Voices

I love words. How full of power they are! What a source of healing, consolation and joy, hope and encouragement they can be for others. People die for lack of words. They can starve just longing for a human voice. . . . I love silence . . . silence and words have been at war within my soul for as long as I can remember. Unfortunately, all too often I have chose words over silence. Silence is scary. It is frightening to be so utterly with yourself . . . In my community we have returned to the practice of Grand Silence beginning at 9 p.m. and continuing until after breakfast the next morning. To be silent alone is one thing, but I have come to love being silent together. To give up words as community is to attempt to go to the depths together.

—Macrina Wiederkehr, o.s.b.
A Tree Full of Angels

Language, used truly, not mere talk, neither pro-
paganda, nor chatter, has real power. Its words are
allowed to be themselves, to bless or curse, wound
or heal. They have the power of a "word made
flesh."

—Kathleen Norris
Amazing Grace: A Vocabulary of Faith

Lonni

There is this friend of mine who is a Benedictine
monk. A little while back I was having a difficult
stretch—illness, betrayal, loss, change, a lot of messy
stuff. I trust and confide in this friend, so he knew all
the complications. I could say to him what I said to no
one else. I depended on him for this. He didn't know it,
but he was holding me together.

During this time, my friend and I had a misunder-
standing. I'm not sure, now, what happened. It seemed
pretty major at the time. In the course of our discus-
sions I barked at him, and I said more than a few ugly
things, sometimes accusingly. Later, when I thought
about my words, I was consumed with fear that I had
destroyed the friendship and he would go away.

My Benedictine friend did not respond with unequivocal calm or detachment to my behavior. I baffled him, and he communicated crisply his annoyance with me. It took us a little while to find time to get together and talk. When we did, he started the conversation with these words:

"Lonni, I know you're scared." He spoke straight—no accusing, blaming, or manipulating. Maybe his words seem rather benign?

Well, you have to understand that no one else ever mentions knowing that I'm scared. Most of the people who love me assume that my fearless disguise is true. Why? Because I spend a lot of energy convincing others that I don't have fears. I suspect a lot of you could say the same.

I am so skilled at weaving the fearless-person-in-charge-of-her-destiny cloak that even those who have loved me longest don't speak out loud of my fear. I tend to withdraw when my fear is revealed. I don't like being busted. Or I lash out, a decidedly disagreeable experience.

My friend didn't hold back. He cut through the tension between us and went for the root of the break in our relationship—my fear that he would turn away from me when he caught sight of my darker side. He didn't use words he learned in Psych 101. He used words for their best purpose—to love, heal, and restore. He used words to move toward me, not away.

His years of striking the balance between silence and words, his years of learning what words are for, his years of learning to honor the power of words have made him incapable of tiptoeing around the truth when it needs saying.

Benedict wants the monk to respect the power of the spoken word. His loathing of, and absolute ban on, grumbling reflects his conviction that words can give life or words can kill. He insists that people choose life.

My friend has the ability to communicate artfully and with few words. What he does say contains a world of meaning beyond the simplicity of his words. This reverence for words is part of the Benedictine tradition. It is a vital lesson for all of us.

Going Inward

Beginning with yourself, select one person each day, for a week, and observe his or her use of words. Remember that your purpose is not to critique but to observe the power in the words, the reactions that words elicit, and the person's awareness of this power.

For one day, try to use half the number of words you would normally use. By doing this, you will be more likely to be sure that every word counts.

Each day, purposefully speak encouraging and positive words to three people with whom you have relatively casual relationships.

Read a book written by an author who is especially gifted with words, for example, Madeleine L'Engle, Frederick Buechner, Walter Wangerin Jr., Walker Percy, Flannery O'Connor, Garrison Keillor.

Eternal Word, you are the giver of all words. You have shaped us in such a way that we can grant life to one another and we can destroy one another with the words we speak. Make me a life-giver. Teach me what words are for. Amen.

28

PLEASURE

The Rule of St. Benedict

Just as there is a wicked zest of bitterness which separates from God . . . so there is a good zeal which separates from evil and leads to God. . . . This, then, is the good kind of zeal which monks must foster with fervent love.

—RB 72:1–3

Other Voices

Why is sex fun? Reproduction certainly doesn't require pleasure. . . . Why is eating fun? Plants and the lower animals manage to obtain their quota of nutrients without the luxury of taste buds. Why can't we? Why are there colors? Some people get along fine without the ability to detect color. . . . Somehow Christians have gotten a reputation as anti-pleasure, and this despite the fact that they believe pleasure was an invention of the Creator himself.

—Philip Yancey
I Was Just Wondering

Lonni

It snowed while I was making a personal retreat at St. Benedict Monastery a couple years ago. A wet, heavy, substantial snow that little boys dream about for sleds, snow forts, and snowball fights. Looking out one of the windows, I noticed Brother John-Martin and Brother Gregory-David, two young monks, shoveling snow and talking quite seriously. Theology. Politics. Philosophy. Spirituality. Exactly the sort of monkly things one would expect. A few moments later I noticed that they were gone and that the snow was not completely shoveled off the sidewalks.

It was a while later, an hour perhaps, that I heard their voices again. I glanced out the window, and there they were—gloriously covered in snow from head to toe, breathing hard, laughing and talking with a certain glee, young faces beaming. I can only imagine what they had been up to. But they reminded me of my five brothers after they had rolled down hills, blasted one another with snowballs, made snow angels, and otherwise gave themselves fully to the pleasure of a snowy day.

Catholics, and monks in particular, are reputed to be against pleasure. This, some would have us believe, is the reason monks give up sex and practice spiritual disciplines that require being tough with themselves. I don't know who these people are who tell us such things, but they obviously don't know much about monks—or Catholicism in general.

Christianity, early on, seemed to be suspicious of pleasure. That attitude came from the intellectuals and philosophers of the day, though, not from Christ. Christ surrounded himself with people whose mouths were stained with wine and kisses, who laughed too loud, who played too hard. Christ himself was once accused of being a party animal (hangs out with crooks and loose women, drinks and eats too much, they said). This suspicion of pleasure still lingers slightly in the air, but it has been banished overwhelmingly to whatever netherworld it came from.

I have received handmade cards and stunningly beautiful candles from Oblate brother Jim, who is serious about his work, his spirituality, and his life at the monastery. The details in these gifts are magnificent, playful, and creative. When he hands me a flower he has grown or a story he has written, there can be no mistaking the pleasure in his eyes. Br. Jim's work, while it might be redundant and difficult at times, gives him pleasure.

I have discovered that the Benedictine experience of pleasure is not smaller or more rigid than mine. It is bigger. It is expansive. It is all-consuming. I have only begun to experience pleasure with the poignancy that my monk friends demonstrate.

There's nothing specifically written about pleasure in Benedict's Rule. Yet Benedict gives one the impression of overall pleasure, and this is articulated by what he says about zeal. Pleasure is also present in the careful handling of tools, the meals in common, the celebrations, and the various acts of hospitality. Benedict expects that the monastic life will not be toil and travail; it will be holy and high pleasure. That's true of our lives outside the monastery, too.

Going Inward

What gives you the most pleasure? Pay attention to your responses to the simple tasks of your day. When do you feel good about yourself? What makes you laugh? When are you proud and content? Do you associate guilt with pleasure? Why?

What gives pleasure to the people you are closest to? Do something that will please someone else.

Look for opportunities to enlighten others about the Christian perspective on pleasure.

Lord, my world drips with pleasures I take for granted. I am grateful for color, for loving touches, for music that reminds me of what is good and what is important. You look up at me from the eyes of a child, and you look down on me from the falling snow. One lifetime is hardly enough time to taste and see how good it all is. Give me the vigor to enjoy and enjoy well. Amen.

29

MARKING TIME

The Rule of St. Benedict

During the winter season, Vigils begins with the verse: *Lord, open my lips and my mouth will proclaim your praise* (Ps. 50 [51]:157).

—*RB 9:1*

From Easter until the first of November, the winter arrangement for the number of psalms is followed. But because summer nights are shorter, the readings from the book are omitted.

—*RB 10:1–2*

On Sunday the monks should arise earlier for Vigils. In these Vigils, too, there must be moderation of quantity.

—*RB 11:1–2*

We believe that the divine presence is everywhere.

—*RB 19:1*

A lamp must be kept burning in the room until morning.

—*RB 22:4*

Other Voices

Who turned on the lights? You did, by waking up: you flipped the light switch, started up the wind machine, kicked on the flywheel that spins the years. Can you catch hold of a treetop, or will you fly off the diving planet as she rolls? Can you ride out the big blow . . . until you fall asleep again, and the winds let up? You will fall asleep again . . . the winds die off, the lights dim, the years slip away as you idle there till you die. . . . Knowing you are alive is feeling the planet buck beneath you, rear, kick and try to throw you. . . . Have you noticed yet that you will die? Do you remember, remember, remember? Then you feel your life as a weekend, a weekend you cannot extend, a weekend in the country.

—Annie Dillard
An American Childhood

For everything there is a season, and a time for every matter under heaven:

a time to be born, and a time to die;

a time to plant, and a time to pluck up what is planted;

a time to kill, and a time to heal;

a time to break down, and a time to build up;

a time to weep, and a time to laugh;

a time to mourn, and a time to dance;

a time to throw away stones, and a time to gather stones together;

a time to embrace, and a time to refrain from embracing;

a time to seek, and a time to lose;

a time to keep, and a time to throw away;

a time to tear, and a time to sew;

a time to keep silence, and a time to speak;

a time to love, and a time to hate;

a time for war, and a time for peace.

. . . That which is, already has been; that which is to be, already is; and God seeks out what has gone by.

—Ecclesiastes 3:1–8, 15

Dan and Lonni

Days, seasons, and years accumulate into a lifetime before we have stretched ourselves fully awake to our world. When experience and maturity finally give us the gift of sight, time counts us down into forever.

The Rule is jammed with passages like the ones above that demonstrate the monastic sense of time and the importance of marking time. Always the voice of Benedict is haunting this sense of time, whispering, "Keep your death before your eyes."

Time is a holy thing. It is mysterious and elusive while being practical and substantial. Because of the ways we measure time and because we coordinate our lives by the passage of time, we can sometimes have an artificial sense of managing time. The truth is that none of us can manage time any more than we can manage a hurricane or manage the seasons or manage God. The Holy One will not be held back by our trembling hands.

We can't control time, but we can mark it. We can carve our initials in it. This is what Benedict understands when he arranges prayer, work, and living to the revolutions of light we call seasons. Rather than trying to manage time, Benedict asks us to embrace it, to walk into it, to hop on the bucking bronco and ride it until our last gasp of air.

In the monastic tradition, time is considered holy; this sense of the sacred is observed every day. The monastic hours of prayer are the basic way in which time is sanctified. The conviction that time is holy is acted upon when the monks stumble to their cold, wooden choir stalls while light creeps up over the hills and again while the sun perches at the sky pinnacle and then again while light crashes into the ridge of night. Again. Again. Relentlessly, time shoves us onward. Relentlessly, the monk hauls himself to prayer. To mark time, Benedict calls his monks to gather and sing the primal prayers that belong to all of us.

Time is not the enemy. It is not the beast to be bridled. Time provides us a place, and the opportunity, to become what we never believed we could be. Time is the vehicle we ride into the great adventure of eternity-not-known. Time holds us upright while carrying us into the lap of God.

Going Inward

Somewhere monastic bells toll the passing of time, lights are turned off, gates are latched, and shades are drawn as night arrives. These little gestures mark our understanding of life as a grace and death as a door. Each of us, monk or not, can find ways to mark time.

Maybe marking time is as simple as being aware that turning on the light in the morning is saying yes to another day and saying yes to God. We enter into the sacred every day. We are often not aware of the ways we do this.

Are you happy with your progress in establishing the spiritual discipline of morning and evening prayer? What other ways can you find to mark time?

God, today I say yes to another day and all its opportunities. Tonight I say thank you for another day and all its opportunities. I am in a cycle of seasons that seems to be taking me somewhere. Help me remember that time is an ally and not an enemy. These seasons that come and go are taking me to you. Give me faith to hold on to that knowledge. Amen.

30

LISTENING
AGAIN

The Rule of St. Benedict

Listen.

—*RB Prologue:1*

Let us get up then, at last, for the Scriptures rouse us. . . .
Let us open our eyes to the light . . . and our ears to the
voice from heaven that every day calls out. . . . *If you hear
his voice today, do not harden your hearts* (Ps. 94 [95]:8).

—*RB Prologue:8–10*

Other Voices

In May of 1995, Bob McNamara of CBS News
reported the unusual story of Judy Daniel's little
yellow duck. The duck was part of a set of plastic
ornaments on her lawn in the small town of
Grapevine, Texas. One day it disappeared and Mrs.
Daniel assumed that it had been carried away by
an animal; but a year later, the plastic duck
returned with a photograph album showing where
it had been. 'The World Quack Tour 94–95' album
contains 43 pictures of the duck's travels: the duck

with a park ranger in St. Louis, by the Rhine, in the Alps, across the Parliament in London, in front of the Eiffel Tower in Paris, at Niagara Falls, and on the beach in Hawaii. . . . The Daniels have no idea how the duck managed all this travel, they have not been able to figure out who might have accompanied it. Reporter McNamara speculated: "Somewhere, someone is enjoying this mystery as much as the Daniels . . ." "Well, the world is full of mystery," added Dan Rather.

Frederic Brussat and Mary Ann Brussat
Spiritual Literacy: Reading the Sacred in Everyday Life

Day to day pours forth speech,
and night to night declares knowledge.

—Psalm 19:2

Lonni and Dan

L isten. Simply, here is the heart of the Rule of St. Benedict. Listen to life. Get out of the front yard, leave the plastic-ornament world, and join the adventure tour. Enter the mystery. God is still able to surprise us. God, after all, is still God, and we are not. The world is indeed full of mystery.

Someone rumbles in the waters of Niagara and the Rhine. Someone drums the beat of the winds and speaks in the rustle of the leaves. There is more than water beating the rhythms of the Great Lakes, and there is more than air and gas whirling in the night sky. *Listen,* Benedict whispers. If you want to hear this Voice, listen.

If we learn nothing else from St. Benedict, he would have us remember this: When the bells ring, listen. When the young speak, listen. Listen to the mantras of the poor. Listen to the baying, the singing, the praying, the mourning, the laughing. When music plays, when night stands still, when loss cuts into your gut, when joy lets you leap over the tallest building in a single bound, pay attention to the moment, to all the moments and all the people and every breath you take beneath the ancient sky.

It would be spiritual apartheid to suggest that God is heard only in monasteries, only among Benedictines, or only through Benedictine spirituality. The Irish speak of a tradition of "thin places." It is believed among us (both authors being of Irish descent) that there are sequestered, sacred spaces on earth where, if you listen very carefully, you can hear God more clearly and feel God more closely than you thought possible.

The metaphor sometimes used for these places is that of a wisp of veiling. Between us and God there seems to exist a wall that hides God and makes us feel often alone. At times, this wall can appear several feet thick and constructed of the sturdiest substance. In thin places, however, the wall is no more than an ethereal veil. Should you press your hand against it, a hand presses back, and should you whisper to it, a Voice answers.

For us, monk and laywoman, a place on a hill in Oxford, Michigan, called St. Benedict Monastery has been and remains a thin place. The tradition of the place, its history and community, the friends, the work, the liturgy, and the ordinariness of it all contribute to making it so.

Make no mistake about it, the secret to discovering thin places is not in finding some coveted geographical location. The secret is inside of us. All the world becomes a thin place, we ourselves become a thin place, as we learn to listen. Listen, St. Benedict calls to us. Listen to every moment. Every day calls out.

Going Inward

Before going to sleep tonight, review the day's events, the people you spoke with, the places you went, and all the sights and sounds of them. In what event did God speak? How did you sense it, or why did you fail to sense it at the time? Make a habit of reminding yourself several times a day to try and be more attentive. It might be as simple as writing "Listen" into some of the empty lines of your planning book or calendar. It is often between the lines and in the empty places where we hear God.

Father, every day does indeed pour forth speech. You are present in all the moments, in the smallest details of my world, in the person I am least inclined to listen to. Take this life I give back to you and make me a thin place for all the others. Keep me always aware of your presence in all the times and places of my life. Amen.

Suggested Reading

Benedictine Resources

Authors' note: Liturgical Press is a publishing house operated by the Benedictines of Collegeville, Minnesota. They have the best selection of Benedictine resources available. Contact them for a catalog. The Liturgical Press, St. John's Abbey, P.O. Box 7500, Collegeville, MN 56321 (1-800-858-5450).

Bianco, Frank. *Voices of Silence: Lives of the Trappists Today.* New York: Paragon House Publishers, 1991. Bianco writes from his experience of living with a community of Trappists (who also live by the Rule of St. Benedict).

Casey, Michael. *The Undivided Heart: The Western Monastic Approach to Contemplation.* Petersham, MS: St. Bede's Publications, 1994.

Chittister, Joan. *Wisdom Distilled from the Daily: Living the Rule of St. Benedict Today.* San Francisco: Harper San Francisco, 1992. Chittister's book contains an excellent section on Lectio.

Cummings, Charles. *Monastic Practices*. Kalamazoo, MI: Cistercian Publications, n.d. This book has an outstanding section on Lectio. Overall, it's an excellent exploration of monasticism that is written for monks and nuns but is also very helpful for laity.

de Waal, Esther. *A Life-Giving Way: A Commentary on the Rule of St. Benedict*. Collegeville, MN: Liturgical Press, 1995. This book is a good choice for anyone interested in learning more about the Rule and Benedict.

Fry, Timothy, ed. *RB 1980: The Rule of St. Benedict*. Collegeville, MN: Liturgical Press, 1981. This comprehensive volume contains the text of the Rule in both Latin and English along with sections on the origin of monasticism, the history of the Rule of St. Benedict, and much more. An inexpensive paperback edition of just the English text of the Rule is also available. The paperback is a compact ninety-six pages long, a size good for briefcase or purse.

Norris, Kathleen. *The Cloister Walk*. New York: Riverhead Books, 1997. Norris writes from her personal experience with Benedictines. Her account is interesting and compelling.

Smith, Cyprian. *The Path of Life: Benedictine Spirituality for Monks and Lay People*. York (U.K.): Ampleforth

Abbey Press, 1995. This book was published in the U.K. Ask your local bookstore to order it.

St. Benedict's Rule for Monks: Selected Passages from the Rule of St. Benedict. Cistercian Studies Series, 99. Kalamazoo, MI: Cistercian Publications, 1994.

Stewart, Columba. *Prayer and Community: The Benedictine Tradition.* Maryknoll, NY: Orbis Books, 1998. This is one of the best books about Benedictine spirituality.

Tvedten, Benet. *A Share in the Kingdom: A Commentary on the Rule of St. Benedict for Oblates.* Collegeville, MN: Liturgical Press, 1989.

Van Houtryve, Dom Idesbalk. *Benedictine Peace.* Translated by Leonard J. Doyle. Westminster, MD: Newman Press, 1950. Van Houtryve's book is out of print but is available in libraries. It's worth the effort to locate the book.

Vest, Norvene. *Friend of the Soul: A Benedictine Spirituality of Work.* [Boston]: Cowley Publications, 1996. Vest's book deals specifically with the topic of work.

Prayer Resources

The Book of Common Worship: Daily Prayer. [Louisville]: Westminster John Knox Press, 1993. This book is very thorough, attractive, and well done. It's a nice portable size. Besides morning and evening prayer, it contains hymns, psalm-tones, prayers, litanies, and a lectionary.

Celebrating Common Prayer: A Version of the Daily Office. Dorchester (U.K.): A. R. Mowbray, 1992. This book is available in leatherflex and hardcover and contains a wealth of resources for morning and evening prayer, as well as daytime and nighttime prayer. It's very thorough and easy to use and contains a full Psalter, which many prayer books do not have. *Celebrating Common Prayer* is one of the best prayer books available.

Christian Prayer: The Liturgy of the Hours. Edition with music. New York: Catholic Book Publishing, 1976. The Daughters of St. Paul also publish an edition of this comprehensive four-week Psalter with all offices of prayer and much more. The book contains substantial seasonal materials. It is a good prayer resource for Catholics who don't want to wrestle with the multivolume *Liturgy of the Hours.*

Huck, Gabe, ed. *Psalms for Morning and Evening Prayer.* [Chicago]: Liturgy Training Publications, 1995. This beautiful book uses the ICEL translation of the Psalms and is arranged according to the Liturgy of Hours.

Morning and Evening Prayer. Farmington, NY: Regina Press, 1974. This is an abridged official version of the Liturgy of the Hours. It's easy to carry with you and contains some seasonal material and hymns.

Sutera, Judith, ed. *Work of God: Benedictine Prayer.* Collegeville, MN: Liturgical Press, 1997. This excellent version of the Liturgy of the Hours is designed with Benedictine oblates in mind. The contributors have used inclusive language. We highly recommend this easy-to-use book, which is portable in size.

Zimmermann, Joyce. *Pray without Ceasing: Prayer for Morning and Evening.* Collegeville, MN: Liturgical Press, 1993. This is a more comprehensive volume than *Work of God.* It includes music and is designed for community use, but it can be used for personal prayer also.

Articles, Papers, and Journals
The American Benedictine Review. This journal is published in March, June, September, and December.

Contact Assumption Abbey, P.O. Box A, Richardton, ND 58652-0901.

"As We Seek God: International Reflections on Contemporary Benedictine Monasticism." Papers presented at the International Symposium, Fifteenth Centenary of Birth of St. Benedict, and published in 1983. This resource is available from Amazon.com.

Dysinger, Luke. "Accepting the Embrace of God: The Ancient Art of Lectio Divina." *Valyermo Benedictine,* spring 1990. This article is available on-line at various prayer and Benedictine sites, including the Order of St. Benedict site, (http://www.osb.org/osb/index.html).

Kline, Francis. "As We Progress in This Life: Ongoing Formation as the Anatomy of Monastic Life." This resource is not in print but is available on-line at the Order of St. Benedict site.

Sisters Today. This journal is published six times a year by Liturgical Press.

"The Spiritual Roots of Society: The Relevance of St. Benedict and His Rule for Contemporary Society." Address given in London to the House of Commons by Cardinal George Basil Hume on July 10, 1996.

The text of the address is available at the Order of St. Benedict site.

Web Sites

Blue Cloud Abbey (http://www.bluecloud.org/psalms.html). This address will take you directly to the page that presents an opportunity to pray the psalms on the same prayer schedule as the male Benedictines at the Blue Cloud Abbey. The schedule is easy to follow; the texts can be printed or downloaded so that you can pray anytime during the day. The text is mostly inclusive.

The Monastery of Christ in the Desert (http://www.christdesert.org/pax.html). This beautiful site is jammed with outstanding art and graphics plus lots of good information about monastic studies, the life of Benedict, the desert fathers, chant, and lots more. It also has readings from the Rule of St. Benedict. This site should be visited if only to see the art.

Mother of God Monastery (http://www.bluecloud.org/nuns.html). This useful Web site contains information about St. Benedict, a good bibliography, and listings of other monasteries.

The Order of St. Benedict (http://www.osb.org/osb/
index.html). This excellent site is updated often with
news, links, and so forth pertaining to all things
Benedictine; it includes readings from the Rule of St.
Benedict, the daily liturgy, and information about
the saint of the day. There is an enormous amount
of information on monastic topics and an excellent
section on St. Benedict, along with bibliographies,
papers, articles, book excerpts, Lectio resources, links
to monasteries, colleges, libraries, personal pages by
monks, an oblate forum, and much more. This is the
top site on the Web for information on Benedictine
monasticism. Bookmark it and come back to it often.
Be sure to click on the hypertext (click on
"Welcome") of Brother Richard's links for the best
all-around selection you'll find anywhere of links
related to religion. The O.S.B. Web site maintains
various directories that will help you find information quickly. Among the most useful are a directory
of monastic E-mail addresses and Web sites and a list
of Benedictine retreat centers. These are more current
than any published directories. If you don't have a
computer or Internet access, check with your local
library.